REAL
LEAN

Understanding the Lean Management System

Bob Emiliani

The Center for Lean Business Management, LLC
Wethersfield, Connecticut

The Center for Lean Business Management, LLC
Wethersfield, CT
Tel: 860.558.7367   www.theclbm.com

Cover design and page layout by Tom Bittel, bittlwrks@aol.com
www.dadsnoisybasement.com

Library of Congress Control Number: 2006910030
Emiliani, M.L., 1958-
     **REAL LEAN: Understanding the Lean Management
     System / M.L. Emiliani**

Includes bibliographical references and index
1. Business 2. Lean management 3. Leadership

I. Title
ISBN-13:   978-0-9722591-1-8
ISBN-10:   0-9722591-1-2

First Edition   January 2007

ORDERING INFORMATION
www.theclbm.com

Made in the U.S.A. using digital print-on-demand technology.

This book is dedicated to its readers, who I
hope are inspired to pursue REAL LEAN.

Preface

This book is a collection of sixteen essays written between 2004 and 2006. Each essay was created with a purpose in mind: To answer specific questions or address confusion that that managers have about Lean management. The essays are written from a practical, not theoretical perspective. They emphasize Lean as a management system, not as group of tools. The essays also emphasize the "Respect for People" principle, which has long been missing from the practice of Lean management.

The "Respect for People" principle has been my strongest area of interest. I first learned how to apply Lean principles and practices in 1994 as a manufacturing manager in the aerospace industry. Within one year, it became apparent to me that the key to successful Lean transformations was being overlooked. So for over twelve years, I have been practicing, studying, and writing on the leadership aspects of Lean management and how to make the "Respect for People" principle come alive. I hope these essays help you comprehend and put into practice this critically important principle for achieving REAL LEAN.

Bob Emiliani
January 2007
Wethersfield, Conn.

Contents

REAL LEAN

1 Keep It REAL

Most of the different forms of Lean that have emerged are actually shortcuts which have caused a great deal of confusion. There is a pressing need to for managers to Keep It REAL!

Over the years, Lean management has taken many different forms, most of which stray far from its original meaning and intent as exemplified by the Toyota Management System. Managers believe they can pick the Lean tools and methods they think are most applicable to their situation, thus creating their own versions of Lean. So while we all use the same word "Lean," it now has many different meanings.

In addition, people at all levels in a company typically misunderstand many Lean principles and practices. For example, it is common to hear people refer to "overprocessing" as one of the seven wastes, when in fact "processing itself" was the waste identified [1]. Another example is andon lights. In some companies, they are used to blame people when a problem arises and levy interdepartmental fines, rather than as a signal to initiate blame-free problem solving activities and improvement.

For these and many other reasons, few companies have been able to achieve notable success despite, in most cases, good intentions and years of implementation effort. A common problem cited by Lean practitioners is backsliding – the reversal of valuable improvements. A root-cause analysis reveals it is due in large part to the failure to understand the role of people in business.

Two broad categories of Lean management practice can be described as REAL LEAN and Fake Lean. Fake Lean is the deployment of only one of the two main principles of Lean – "Continuous Improvement" – and typically just the tools. Everyone loves the tools. They are easy to understand and use, and they work. If that were all Lean is, there would be hundreds of big success stories – but instead there are only a few.

Managers often see Lean as one or more of the following:

- A program or initiative
- Tools for the manager's tool kit
- A way to eliminate workers
- A way to increase stock price
- Something to do only in operations

They can only be practicing Fake Lean. Why? Because they do not recognize the second principle, "Respect for People" [2]. It is this second principle that makes the first principle "Continuous Improvement" possible. As a result, opportunities to significantly improve the entire business system – vs. isolated or point optimization – and develop the human resources in it, are lost.

Only recently has the second principle, "Respect for People," been made explicit [3,4]. However, astute Lean management practitioners have implicitly known about this all along [5]. For example, in Fake Lean practice, a frequent outcome of productivity improvement is layoffs. This is inconsistent with the "Respect for People" principle, and undercuts participation in future continuous improvement activities. It is not surprising the business press – and many workers – regularly refer to Lean as "mean."

REAL LEAN is the simultaneous deployment of both principles – "Continuous Improvement" and "Respect for People." But what is "Respect for People?" The words sound simple enough, and just about every senior manager says: "Oh yeah, we do that; it's a given." As it turns out, they don't do it, and it is not a given. Putting "Respect for People" into practice isn't so easy because there are deeper levels of meaning that must be confronted and thoroughly understood.

Conventional leadership behaviors, business tools, reporting systems, and business metrics are, with rare exception, inconsistent with the "Respect for People" principle. For example, we all know standard costs, earned hours, and purchase price variance metrics drive batch-and-queue thinking, firefighting, and the blame game. Yet these metrics remain firmly embedded in information systems and continue to be used in daily management of companies that also claim to be Lean.

Unfortunately, many people think REAL LEAN is an idealistic and therefore impractical approach to the Lean transformation. Having this view means no action will be taken to improve. We need only to look at the long-term financial and non-financial performance of Toyota Motor Corporation and The Wiremold Company (in the period from 1991 to 2001), for example, to know with certainty that deploying both "Continuous Improvement" and "Respect for People" yields much better outcomes. It also creates much more effective leaders [6,7,8] and a strong internal leadership bench.

So should you be concerned if your company is doing is Fake Lean? The answer is: Yes you should! The reasons why are as follows:

- Fake Lean – using just the tools – is easy for your competitors to replicate. Thus, your competitive advantage, if any is achieved, will be fleeting. REAL LEAN is much harder for competitors to copy.

- With Fake Lean, the rate of improvement is low. Does your competitive environment allow you the luxury of improving slowly?

- Fake Lean can do more harm than good because management's approach to improvement is not clear. It is a mix of Lean and non-Lean principles, practices, and metrics. This creates confusion, and most people will lose interest and disengage.

- Many people have the view that some improvement is better than no improvement. However, deploying Lean incorrectly from the start will undermine future Lean efforts. The errors will have to be undone, and that's rework. It will take time, effort, and money to correct the errors – resources you might not have.

- Fake Lean is a not a good learning experience. Learning the wrong things perpetuates damaging practices and misconceptions, and leads to poor long-term results.

- Deploying Fake Lean demonstrates disrespect for people – employees, suppliers, customers, investors, and the community.

- REAL LEAN results in much better financial and non-financial performance compared to Fake Lean.

Managers engaged in Fake Lean typically blame rising costs on external factors, such as healthcare, when the actual problem is that they are unaware of the "Respect for People" principle.

Most people come to work every day to do good things, and not make situations worse. But this is exactly what happens when managers disregard the "Respect for People" principle.

Notes

[1] T. Ohno, *Toyota Production System*, Productivity Press, Portland, OR, 1988, p. 19

[2] The word "People" in "Respect for People" means key stakeholders such as associates (management and non-management), suppliers, customers, investors, and the community.

[3] Toyota Motor Corporation, "The Toyota Way 2001," internal document, Toyota City, Japan, April 2001

[4] J.K. Liker, *The Toyota Way*, McGraw Hill, New York, NY, 2004

[5] B. Emiliani, with D. Stec, L. Grasso, and J. Stodder, *Better Thinking, Better Results: Case Study and Analysis of an Enterprise-Wide Lean Transformation, Second Edition*, The CLBM, LLC, Wethersfield, Conn., 2007

[6] M.L. Emiliani and D.J. Stec, "Using Value Stream Maps to Improve Leadership," *Leadership and Organizational Development Journal*, Vol. 25, No. 8, pp. 622-645, 2004

[7] M.L. Emiliani, "Linking Leaders' Beliefs to Their Behaviors and Competencies," *Management Decision*, Vol. 41, No. 9, pp. 893-910, 2003.

[8] M.L. Emiliani, "Lean Behaviors," *Management Decision*, Vol. 36, No. 9, pp. 615-631, 1998.

2 Improving Your Lean Transformation

*The truth is, most companies have great difficulty
achieving a Lean transformation.
Avoid eleven common errors, and you will improve!*

In 2003 we published the Shingo Prize-winning book *Better Thinking, Better Results*, which describes The Wiremold Company's enterprise-wide Lean transformation between 1991 and 2001. Since then we have wanted to write another book telling the story of an excellent Lean transformation in a different manufacturing business, or in a service business. But so far, we have not found anything to write about. Perhaps it is because most Lean transformations are still early in the process.

While thousands of companies world-wide have embraced Lean over the last 20 years, only a few have applied Lean management across the enterprise. The good news is that many manufacturing businesses are starting to apply Lean principles and practices to processes other than in operations, such as engineering, procurement, or accounting, but not yet to human resources, MIS, legal, sales, marketing, etc. Senior managers at many services businesses are beginning to realize Lean principles and practices also apply to their business – though mainly in operations.

There are widespread misunderstandings about Lean among senior managers, which has in turn led to many faulty Lean transformations. Not surprisingly, many workers then think of Lean as nothing more than a "flavor of the month." Layoffs after productivity improvements have been achieved only harden the bad perceptions.

Layoffs are not the intent of the Lean, and nobody should lose their job due to productivity improvement. Instead, the focus should be on positive improvement and stable long-term growth. Positive improvement results in better financial and non-financial performance, job stabilization or job creation, higher quality and lower cost products and services, better relationships between key stakeholders such as employees, suppliers, customers, investors, and the community , and thus more competitive manufacturing or service businesses.

While progress has been made in recent years, the full bene-fits of Lean have yet to be realized by most companies and their end-use customers. There is a high level of awareness of Lean in many organizations, yet knowledge of Lean as a man-agement system among senior managers is very low. In addi-tion, most senior managers overstate their company's Lean capabilities and progress, which is consistent with their limit-ed understanding of Lean, the common tendency to mix Lean and non-Lean business practices and metrics, and lack of direct participation in continuous improvement activities.

The Lean management system has two key principles: "Continuous Improvement" and "Respect for People" [1]. "Continuous Improvement" is the tools and methods used to improve productivity, while "Respect for People" embodies leadership behaviors and business practices that must be con-sistent with efforts to eliminate waste and create value for end-use customers. Unfortunately, most managers implement only "Continuous Improvement" and do not implement both

"Continuous Improvement" and "Respect for People." If they see it at all, "Respect for People" is incorrectly understood as adding cost, when in fact it reduces costs. Consequently, the pace of Lean transformation is slow, and only modest levels of improvement are achieved.

We have observed many errors in how senior managers go about implementing Lean. They include:

- **Management System.** Senior managers typically understand Lean as a "manufacturing thing," and not as a comprehensive management system. Thus, the application of Lean principles and practices is limited to only a portion of the company's activities such as operations. That, of course, makes no sense, since there is waste in every business process.

- **Leadership Behaviors.** These remain deeply rooted in batch-and-queue thinking, which greatly conflicts with efforts to implement Lean principles and practices [2]. In other words, senior managers often exhibit wasteful behaviors [3], while at the same time telling workers to eliminate waste. People notice this inconsistency, and silently question senior management's commitment to Lean.

- **Leadership Participation.** Every senior manager we talk to says they support Lean, but in reality they believe they should be doing other things, or claim they are too busy to get involved with kaizen – either as facilitators or as team members. As the saying goes, "talk is cheap." The lack of personal participation in improvement activities sends the wrong message, and leaders miss important opportunities to deepen their understanding of Lean. It is another source of inconsistency that results in questions about senior management's commitment to Lean.

- **Management Turnover.** It is impossible to achieve a Lean transformation with high management turnover. Senior managers that come and go every few years can not learn the Lean management system, or they introduce tools, methods, or metrics that conflict with Lean principles and practices. In cases where the Lean transformation has been most successful, there is long-term stability in the senior management team.

- **Business Metrics.** Financial and non-financial metrics usually remain rooted in batch-and-queue thinking, which conflicts with efforts to implement Lean principles and practices. We see many examples of beautiful one-piece flow cells that are measured to both takt time and the batch-and-queue metric "earned hours." Invariably, the metric that matters most is earned hours, thus trumping efforts to respond to actual customer demand. This violates the "Respect for People" principle – specifically, respect for employees, suppliers, customers, and investors.

- **Layoffs.** The result of productivity improvement is often unemployment, which impedes worker participation in future improvement activities. This outcome is inconsistent with Lean because it too violates the "Respect for People" principle. Not surprisingly, the pace of improvement is greatly slowed.

- **Strategy Integration.** In most cases, Lean activities do not directly link to corporate strategy and goals. Kaizen is often applied haphazardly; fantastic improvements are achieved in activities that mean nothing to the company or its end-use customers. Some companies are beginning to address this by using hoshin kanri (i.e. policy deployment).

- **Total Cost.** Senior managers typically do not understand the "total cost" of a purchase – just purchase price. They use purchasing tools that are inconsistent with Lean principles and practices such as economic order quantities and reverse auctions [4]. Price-based metrics such as purchase price variance (PPV) promote destructive power-based bargaining with suppliers. This undercuts efforts to practice collaborative problem solving with suppliers.

- **Time Horizon.** It is common for senior managers to be focused on the short-term. The Lean transformation requires management to focus on the long-term, without losing sight of important short- and mid-term goals. Most senior managers will tell you they care a lot about the future of the company, yet they unintentionally behave in ways and cling to metrics that strongly reinforce short-term thinking.

- **Focus.** Most senior managers of publicly owned businesses are obsessively focused on shareholders, and usually make decisions that come at the expense of other stakeholders such as employees or suppliers. It is impossible to achieve a Lean transformation with shareholders as the singular focus. Instead, managers must balance the interests of key stakeholders, which, if done correctly, yields better results for shareholders [5]. Successful Lean transformations have a proper focus on end-use customers, which are the primary source of cash flow that investors care most about.

* **Supply Chain.** It is difficult for suppliers to practice Lean effectively if their customers do not. Applying Lean throughout a supply chain requires the sponsorship and participation of large buying organizations that correctly apply Lean principles and practices to their own internal activities [6]. Most companies practice variations of Lean that contain many flaws, thus making the "train-the-trainer" approach to implementing Lean in supply chains ineffective. Managers who are serious about Lean quickly abandon power-based bargaining and price-based purchasing metrics.

Without question, there is much room for improvement.

Senior managers who do not understand the Lean management system or its intent are not hopeless "concrete heads." Rather, most are valuable resources who can be shown how to improve their leadership and business skills if they are willing to learn new things – many of which will be at odds with what they previously learned on-the-job or in business school.

The Lean management system is a truly fabulous creation. Implemented correctly, it makes work fun, exciting, and much more fulfilling. It also leads to the kinds of favorable business outcomes that senior managers seek. That will be something special to write about!

Notes

[1] Toyota Motor Corporation, "The Toyota Way 2001," internal document, Toyota City, Japan, April 2001.

[2] M.L. Emiliani, "Linking Leaders' Beliefs to Their Behaviors and Competencies," *Management Decision*, Vol. 41, No. 9, pp. 893-910, 2003.

[3] M.L. Emiliani, "Lean Behaviors," *Management Decision*, Vol. 36, No. 9, 1998, pp. 615-631.

[4] M.L. Emiliani, "Sourcing in the Global Aerospace Supply Chain Using Online Reverse Auctions," *Industrial Marketing Management*, Vol. 33, pp. 65-72, 2004.

[5] B. Emiliani, with D. Stec, L. Grasso, and J. Stodder, *Better Thinking, Better Results: Case Study and Analysis of an Enterprise-Wide Lean Transformation, Second Edition*, The CLBM, Wethersfield, Conn., 2007.

[6] J. Dyer and K. Nobeoka, "Creating and Managing a High-Performance Knowledge Sharing Network: The Toyota Case," *Strategic Management Journal*, Vol. 21, pp. 345-367, 2000.

3 The Great Misunderstanding

Our knowledge of Lean has come to us in pieces over time. As a result, most people today recognize Lean as simply a set of tools to help drive improvement. This is a great misunderstanding.

In the 25 years or so since people outside of Toyota first started to become familiar with Lean, it has been interesting to witness incremental acceptance of Lean from department to department, company to company, and industry to industry. Today, the wide-ranging benefits of Lean are well known and beyond any question [1].

A significant barrier that prevents top managers from fully comprehending the magnitude and breadth of the wide-ranging benefits is their view of Lean. Most continue to understand Lean as a tool kit, a program, or an initiative based on a set of tools. Thinking of Lean this way prevents corporations from better satisfying their end-use customers and achieving much more favorable financial and non-financial results.

In the search for the next big thing, it is increasingly common to find marriages of continuous improvement methods. It's easy to do because they usually share one or more common objectives, such as reducing variation. One such marriage combines the words Lean and six sigma, and is marketed to corporate customers under many different trade names.

Unfortunately, it makes no sense to pair Lean and six sigma together as equals. Why? Because Lean is a management system [2], and six sigma is a tool. It is akin to marrying an auto-mobile and a unicycle, because they have transportation or human operators in common. But the two are vastly different in design, functionality, and impact on users and the environment.

To make this distinction clear, we must first understand the difference between a system and a tool. A system is an organized and consistent set of principles and related practices that are broadly applied to any situation. A tool is an instrument or means to assist in the performance of a specific activity or operation. A tool could be used in the absence of any system, in conflict with a system, or in harmony with a system.

Of course there are many important and useful tools that support the Lean management system, including six sigma. Each tool helps people understand the true nature of a problem so that countermeasures can be applied. Most are simple, easy to learn, and effective.

We must also think about what a principle is, and why principles are important in the strategic and daily management of organizations. A principle is a basic, inviolate rule that governs decision-making and the conduct of day-to-day activities.

Practicing Lean in the absence of the "Respect for People" principle [3] means it would be acceptable for management to lay off workers who have participated in productivity improvement [4], or squeeze suppliers using tools such as reverse auctions. Leaders who practice the "Respect for People" principle would not do these things.

A conundrum is that the marketplace – senior managers who

buy Lean training – wants tools [5]. They think the management system they learned on-the-job or in business school is
the one best way, and that it can be improved simply by
adding several new continuous improvement tools to their
tool kit.

There is obviously a weakness in business education and
leadership thinking and practice when it fails to inquire and
understand the true nature of something – in this case, the
Lean management system.

Consider the following analogy: To build a house you need an
architect to design it and create blueprints, a general contractor to manage construction, and trades people to construct it
using tools. Thinking of Lean as a "tool kit" ignores the
important roles of the architect (i.e. top management) and
general contractor (i.e. middle management) – as well as the
need for their involvement – and only recognizes the existence and contributions of the trades people – i.e. associates.

To construct a Lean company, you need an architect, general
contractor, and trades people working together, every day.
They must all participate if one expects to be successful. The
trades people can not do it alone, but that is what they are
being asked to do.

Thinking of Lean as a nothing more than a tool kit helps
explain why most senior managers do not participate directly
in activities such as policy deployment, kaizen, the creation
of visual controls, root cause analysis, etc.

Assigning construction of a Lean company to associates at

lower levels using only the tools will result in efforts that lack focus and are decoupled from corporate strategy. To avoid falling short of expectations, there needs to be a blueprint and focused daily activities that turn the blueprint into reality.

Unfortunately, what we see happening almost all the time is dedicated Lean efforts that do not result in much improvement – despite claims made by managers of great progress. It is common to hear people say how difficult it is to "become Lean" [6] or express concern over losing the gains they have made.

Most Fortune 500 companies are applying Lean and six sigma, either alone or in combination, in one or more parts of their business. The top leaders of these companies – as well as non-profit organizations such as government and hospitals – would do well to understand the dramatic differences between the two. It would help them avoid falling prey to other tempting misunderstandings [7] that, in the end, will undermine well-intentioned efforts necessary to create value for end-use customers and prosper in competitive environments.

So what should managers do if they are heavily invested in six sigma but now want to adopt the Lean management system? The solution is easy, and hard. Associates and mid-level managers will buy into Lean if management simply admits they misunderstood Lean and six sigma. However, most managers are unwilling to admit errors [8], despite the fact that doing so is a key indicator of good leadership. And they will have a difficult time explaining the misunderstanding if they do not correctly grasp the intent of Lean and its many nuances and interconnections.

Practicing Lean management requires managers to question everything, including what they learned in expensive and prestigious MBA programs. Some managers have no problem letting go of knowledge that does not serve them, their company, or their customers well. They give it up in an instant. Most others will steadfastly cling to their knowledge because it is a trusty, well-understood, and comfortable anchor. But it is just that – an anchor; dead weight on the heart and mind.

Managers who can not let go must critically question their own communications and directives. Managers tell people they must adapt to change and learn new things because it will help them prosper as individuals and as well as the company. Another important leadership competency is consistency, and people know very quickly when management is not consistent. If leaders are serious about improvement, then they must do many things they do not really want to do, or have not given much thought to doing, just like everyone else.

Senior managers often say how much they care about the company and its customers. If that is true, then pursuing Lean should be an easy decision. Explaining misunderstandings is uncomfortable, but necessary. Associates will respect managers for reducing confusion, and this will help build trust [9] – which is a key requirement for achieving a successful Lean transformation.

Notes

[1] B. Emiliani, with D. Stec, L. Grasso, and J. Stodder, *Better Thinking, Better Results: Case Study and Analysis of an Enterprise-Wide Lean Transformation, Second Edition*, The CLBM, LLC, Wethersfield, Conn., 2007.

[2] Y. Monden, *Toyota Management System*, Productivity Press, Portland, OR, 1993

[3] Toyota Motor Corporation, "The Toyota Way 2001," internal document, Toyota City, Japan, April 2001.

[4] Laying people off as a result of continuous improvement activities is the *greatest* misunderstanding that senior managers have about Lean – and is clearly inconsistent with the "Respect for People" principle.

[5] In most cases corporate customers want tools, and there are hundreds of Lean consultants happy to supply the tools. But a few years later, senior managers often wonder why the tools or program failed or fell short of expectations. That is because tools alone are never enough. They must be accompanied by a broader system of management principles and leadership practices consistent with the management principles. See M.L. Emiliani and D.J. Stec, "Using Value Stream Maps to Improve Leadership," *Leadership and Organizational Development Journal*, Vol. 25, No. 8, pp. 622-645, 2004.

[6] As you may already know, Lean is a journey, not an end-point. You never "become lean."

[7] Another important misunderstanding about Lean is: "The only reason to do Lean is to make more money!" That is a greedy and selfish rationale, inconsistent with the both the "Continuous Improvement" and "Respect for People" principles. Making more money is one of the many positive outcomes of successful application of the Lean management system, not the prime objective.

[8] Toyota expresses this as "Learning from Mistakes: We view errors as opportunities for learning." From "The Toyota Way 2001," Toyota Motor Corporation, internal document, Toyota City, Japan, April 2001, p. 7.

[9] Toyota expresses this as "Mutual trust and mutual responsibility." From "The Toyota Way 2001," Toyota Motor Corporation, internal document, Toyota City, Japan, April 2001, p.10. See also *The Toyota Way* by J.L. Liker, McGraw-Hill, New York, NY, 2004, pp. 74-78

4 Improving Leadership in Lean Businesses

It's time for leaders to complement thinking Lean with learning how to behave Lean. Putting the two together will accelerate your Lean transformation and lead to far better results.

The automotive industry is a good example of what happens when companies get good at applying only Lean tools: they achieve only half of the financial and non-financial benefits of Lean. Similar limited results are also common in service businesses, non-profit, and government organizations. This has led some managers to realize there is a leadership dimension specific to Lean that they do not understand and need to address.

Leaders who understand Lean well realize the reason to implement Lean is not purely financial. After all, a company's inventory turns and cash flow figures are not a rallying point that end-use customers care about. The better reason for implementing Lean is to eliminate waste and increase value for end-use customers, which leads to better financial and non-financial performance.

In the most general sense, the Lean management system seeks to get information to flow without interruption, whether the information looks like a part, is a document, or verbal communication between people. Talking the narrow view that Lean is simply a means to get materials to flow is short-sighted. Value stream maps, after all, show us that we need to get both material and information to flow.

Lean leaders who recognize and apply both Lean principles, "Continuous Improvement" and "Respect for People" [1], enjoy much better outcomes. However, it is not enough to have an intellectual understanding of these two principles. Their meaning must be understood at much deeper levels, which only occurs though regular participation in kaizen. Managers who do not participate in kaizen will find it difficult, if not impossible, to lead a Lean transformation successfully. The business will surely realize some improvements, but the best possible outcome that can be achieved is to stay even with all the other competitors out there who are focused solely on Lean tools.

The "Respect for People" principle has long been unrecognized, ignored, or misunderstood by most senior managers. Why is that? One way managers like to learn about Lean is through shop or office tours. However, it is very difficult to see the "Respect for People" principle in operation during brief walk-throughs. So managers simply miss it. Returning to the automotive industry example, this explains why Toyota's competitors, focused on deploying only Lean tools – partly as a result of many factory tours – have had very limited success. "Respect for People" is the principle which enables continuous improvement, and it is the much bigger challenge.

The "Respect for People" principle became widely apparent only in 2001, when Toyota published an internal document titled "The Toyota Way 2001" [2]. This was a principal focus of our book, *Better Thinking, Better Results* [3]. However, astute Lean leaders have known all along that they also have to practice "Respect for People." How did they know this?

They knew it from two sources:

- Their direct participation in kaizen
- Reading books by Taiichi Ohno and other former Toyota executives

Unfortunately, most people read Ohno's book, *Toyota Production System* [4], with interest in knowing only about Lean tools.

Since 2001, I have used Ohno's book in a graduate course on Lean leadership [5]. At first, students can not understand why such a book was assigned. They think to themselves: "This is a leadership course, not a manufacturing course." They are expecting to read a book titled: *Become A Great Leader In 14 Days or Less!* Student's initial expectation is to quickly obtain the secret formula for effective leadership. Instead, they read *Toyota Production System* from a different viewpoint: for the many important things Ohno has to say about leadership, not production.

Students, most of whom work in service organizations and know nothing about manufacturing, soon realize that Ohno's book is a great leadership book. Every semester I ask students if *Toyota Production System* should remain as required reading, or should it be dropped in favor of a traditional leadership book. The response, from hundreds of students, has been unanimous: keep Ohno's book in the curriculum. Students' reaction to Ohno's book is extremely positive, and every student says they have no intention to sell the book back to the bookstore when the course is over. It's a keeper. They want to have it to read again and again so they can gain new insights and additional leadership inspiration.

Since 1998, my co-authors and I have written several practical papers that describe what leaders must do differently if they expect to achieve a successful Lean transformation. We show the difference between traditional leadership routines and what effective Lean leaders do, and also give many deep insights into what "Respect for People" really means.

The first paper, titled "Lean Behaviors" [6], built upon what Ohno said: There are two types of work – value-added and non-value added but necessary work – and waste. Ohno's focus was the task component of work. But to get the value-added work to flow without interruption, there is also a behavioral component of work. After all, it is people who do or don't do the work that end-use customers pay for.

The paper describes two types of leadership behaviors – value-added and non-value added but necessary behaviors [7] – and waste. Behavioral waste is defined as behaviors that do not add value and can be eliminated. Examples of wasteful leadership behaviors include: stereotypes, bullying, inaccessibility, fomenting confusion, office politics, unknown expectations, saying one thing and doing another, inability to admit errors, and blaming people for problems. Such behaviors add cost but do not add any value. No end-use customer wants to pay for the delays and re-work caused by wasteful leadership behaviors.

Leaders who tell associates to eliminate waste in processes must be totally consistent and not behave in wasteful ways. It just makes sense. In addition, leaders who adopt Lean but continue to behave in wasteful ways violate the "Respect for

People" principle. Extending Ohno's definitions of work and waste to the realm of leadership and leadership behaviors is simplicity itself. It is an utterly practical solution to an enormous problem – but only if leaders understand what waste is. Again, to get that understanding they must participate in kaizen.

Another paper titled "Continuous Personal Improvement" [8] shows how the exact same tools that Lean businesses use to improve processes can also be used to improve leadership. This results in an approach to leadership development that is simple and completely consistent with Lean principles and practices.

The paper "Linking Leader's Beliefs to their Behaviors and Competencies" [9] shows how traditional leadership competency models do not result in any substantive changes in leadership behaviors because they fail to address managers' fundamental beliefs about the practice of business [10]. A practical method was created to illustrate how a conventional leader's beliefs lead to behaviors, which in turn lead to competencies that most managers would find undesirable. It then shows how the beliefs, behaviors, and competencies of leaders skilled in the Lean management system are remarkably different and much better aligned with the favorable outcomes that managers seek. Once again, kaizen is the key. To change their beliefs, senior managers must participate in many kaizens.

The paper "Using Value Stream Maps to Improve Leadership" [11] presents for the first time how value stream maps can be used to determine leadership beliefs, behaviors, and competencies. Current and future state value stream maps for manufacturing and service business processes illustrate the progression from belief to behavior to competency. The beliefs, behaviors, and competencies of leaders skilled in conventional and Lean management thinking and practice are shown to be very different. The big deal about this paper is that it presents a high impact, practical, simple, and much less expensive route for identifying leadership problems and improving leadership effectiveness using diagrams and language that Lean people already understand.

Interest in improving leadership in Lean businesses is increasing, and some senior managers are beginning to recognize that effective Lean leaders are different. What they do not yet understand is the path for improving leadership, which differs greatly from the conventional approaches they are familiar with. It turns out that improving leadership for Lean businesses is actually much simpler. The impact on associates, suppliers, customers, and investors will be nothing but favorable – if senior managers are willing to learn and do new things. The goods news is that it will be a lot of fun.

Lastly, consider the profile of an effective Lean leader that we have discovered:

- A person who reads – committed to lifelong learning
- Wants to try what he or she read – curious, seeks to validate the reading
- Persistent – failure means understand the root cause and try again and again
- Never stops thinking – problems are a value-laden personal challenge
- Constantly communicating – likes to teach others
- Totally consistent and disciplined – variation in leader-

ship is waste
- Concerned about cause-effect relationships – both task and behavioral
- Humble and participative – not smarter than everyone else and has much to learn

So here is the homework assignment for senior managers: continue to learn about Lean management by reading the premiere books and papers and, most importantly, regularly participate in kaizen.

Notes

[1] The words sound simple, but putting "Respect for People" into practice is not. It takes years to understand this principle deeply, particularly in relation to business performance metrics, enterprise software systems, and financial analyses.

[2] Toyota Motor Corporation, "The Toyota Way 2001," internal document, Toyota City, Japan, April 2001.

[3] B. Emiliani, with D. Stec, L. Grasso, and J. Stodder, *Better Thinking, Better Results: Case Study and Analysis of an Enterprise-Wide Lean Transformation, Second Edition*, The CLBM, LLC, Wethersfield, Conn., 2007.

[4] T. Ohno, *Toyota Production System*, Productivity Press, Portland, OR, 1988.

[5] This course is highly rated by students partly because I apply Lean principles and practices to course design and delivery. How I achieve this is described in my paper: "Improving Business School Courses by Applying Lean Principles and Practices," *Quality Assurance in Education*, Vol. 12, No. 4, pp. 175-187, 2004.

[6] M.L. Emiliani, "Lean Behaviors," *Management Decision*, Vol. 36, No. 9, pp. 615-631, 1998.

[7] Non-value added but necessary behaviors can also be thought of as unavoidable behaviors, since people are not perfect.

[8] M.L. Emiliani, "Continuous Personal Improvement," *Journal of Workplace Learning*, Vol. 10, No. 1, pp. 29-38, 1998.

[9] M.L. Emiliani, "Linking Leaders' Beliefs to Their Behaviors and Competencies," *Management Decision*, Vol. 41, No. 9, pp. 893-910, 2003.

[10] Traditional leadership competency models do not consider manager's beliefs. The models assume all managers share the same beliefs. Thus the starting point for improvement is behaviors, not beliefs, and is thus fundamentally flawed.

[11] M.L. Emiliani and D.J. Stec, "Using Value Stream Maps to Improve Leadership," *Leadership and Organizational Development Journal*, Vol. 25, No. 8, pp. 622-645, 2004.

5 Creating a Lean Culture

Creating a Lean culture seems very difficult.
But it does not have to be that way.

"How do we create a Lean culture?" That is a question we often hear from managers and associates. For years this has been a prime concern of many Lean practitioners. However, focusing on Lean culture as "the answer" can impede people's ability to gain a deeper understanding of the Lean management system and how to improve. Said another way, searching for the secret to creating Lean culture can become a harmful distraction.

Consider a rock-and-roll band. To make good music, each band member must possess several important characteristics:

- Have a burning interest
- Be highly motivated
- Deeply committed
- Hungry to learn various technical and non-technical aspects
- Practice relentlessly to gain mastery
- Develop discipline to sustain daily practice
- Not forget what they learned in practice when it is time to perform

They must also set realistic but achievable goals, and also be sensible – such as stop doing things which do not help meet the goals. While a band might not become world-famous, band members will likely have a lot of fun along the way.

They will also encounter some frustrations, as success usually does not come easily. However, bands that do these seven things make it look easy to those of us who have no idea of time and effort they put in to making good music. Is this the culture of rock bands?

You can easily replace the word "band" with the word "company," and see that the same things would apply if a company wants to become successful in their efforts to practice Lean management. Organizations that practice Lean management well do not possess a mystical culture. Instead, it is the people – the "band members" – who do these seven things.

However, it is common to find managers:

- With an interest in Lean, but not a burning interest
- Motivated, but not highly motivated
- Committed, but not deeply committed
- Interested in learning, but not hungry to learn
- Who practice periodically, but not relentlessly
- Are disciplined when they are in the mood, but not every day
- And forget what they learned in practice when business conditions change

Rather than searching for a secret formula, it is better to just do kaizen – the process for continuous improvement that is practiced daily by people at all levels in an organization [1]. Participating in kaizen is the key activity which leads to the formation of new beliefs which are the foundation for creating a Lean culture [2,3]. It is also very important to stop doing things that do not help an organization achieve its goal of creating a Lean culture, such as continued use of policies and metrics that contradict Lean principles and practices.

In the companies that practice Lean well, there is a clear and consistent pattern among managers and associates who have a strong desire to succeed, and also skillfully practice both Lean principles: "Continuous Improvement" and "Respect for People" [4].

The many benefits of Lean management, practiced correctly, are undeniable [5]. Without the seven characteristics, it will be difficult to create a Lean culture and the best examples of Lean management practice will be few. The good news for those who succeed is a much brighter future, built on a customer-first foundation.

There is some good news for companies who are not having much success: they can become more successful – though it may require the Board of Directors to intervene and ensure most of the top managers possess the seven characteristics we have described. The question is: How will they know?

It turns out that in most cases, they don't, and so unfortunately something bad happens. Often the people who get promoted within the first year or two after starting the Lean transformation are the ones with the poorest understanding of Lean principles and practices – though they are usually able to talk a good line. They tend to be people who can reliably make-the-month the old-fashioned way, and thus help the CEO and CFO stay out of trouble.

Top managers often say Lean is critical to the company's

future. If Lean is truly critical, then the leading candidates for advancement should be the people who understand Lean management best. And the talent pool will be among those who regularly participate in kaizen. Promoting the right people will motivate others who do not understand Lean to learn and improve.

Implementing Lean means top managers and Directors must make a clear shift away from tired political-based promotion practices that favor the "good old boys and girls," to a truer meritocracy that advances those who understand and implement Lean very well. Indeed, this is exactly what happens in companies whose managers possess a very deep understanding of Lean. They recognize that saying one thing – *we must eliminate waste* – and doing another – *promoting people who don't know how to eliminate waste* – is variation; a wasteful inconsistent behavior that adds cost (e.g. causes people to disengage or actively subvert Lean efforts) and does not add value [6]. This is one of many very important aspects of the Lean transformation which are not well understood by most senior managers [7].

In summary, successful efforts to create a Lean culture are preceded by the seven characteristics. Further, it is essential to improve the criteria for advancement and also ensure that promotion processes are consistent with Lean principles and practices. Doing so would clearly support efforts to create a Lean culture.

Notes

[1] Always remember to apply the three principles of kaizen: process and results; system focus; non-blaming/non-judgmental. Source: M. Imai, "Kaizen Seminar", Hartford Graduate Center, Hartford, Conn., May 1988.

[2] M.L. Emiliani, "Linking Leaders' Beliefs to Their Behaviors and Competencies," *Management Decision*, Vol. 41, No. 9, pp. 893-910, 2003.

[3] M.L. Emiliani and D.J. Stec, "Using Value Stream Maps to Improve Leadership," *Leadership and Organizational Development Journal*, Vol. 25, No. 8, pp. 622-645, 2004.

[4] Toyota Motor Corporation, "The Toyota Way 2001," internal document, Toyota City, Japan, April 2001.

[5] B. Emiliani, with D. Stec, L. Grasso, and J. Stodder, *Better Thinking, Better Results: Case Study and Analysis of an Enterprise-Wide Lean Transformation, Second Edition*, The CLBM, LLC, Wethersfield, Conn., 2007.

[6] M.L. Emiliani, "Lean Behaviors," *Management Decision*, Vol. 36, No. 9, pp. 615-631, 1998.

[7] M.L. Emiliani and D.J. Stec, "Leaders Lost in Transformation," *Leadership and Organizational Development Journal*, Vol. 26, No. 5, pp. 370-387, 2005.

6 Lean is Music to My Ears

*There are many remarkable similarities between
Lean management and music. Understanding this can
deepen our appreciation of the sensibility and
practicality of Lean management – and hopefully
motivate senior managers to strengthen their
efforts to practice and learn more.*

Why is it there are so few top managers who are good at leading Lean transformations? After all, it has been nearly 30
years since the first accounts of Toyota's production system
were reported in the manufacturing trade press, about twenty
years since Productivity Press began selling their translations
of works by Taiichi Ohno and Shigeo Shingo, and about 15
years since Lean has been reported on in the national business
press. And soon it will be 20 years since Shingijutsu Co. Ltd.
consultants started teaching the Toyota Production System to
U.S. managers.

Lean management is not theoretical or governed by complex
mathematical equations. While the principles are somewhat
challenging to fully understand, the tools and processes are
simple and very effective which is why most people focus on
those. So what's the problem?

It seems that being good at implementing Lean principles and
practices requires basic capabilities which few senior managers possess. Could the reasons for this be similar to why
few managers play musical instruments?

As I have learned more and more about Lean management over the years, I am struck by the many similarities between Lean and music. Specifically, how one learns to play music in comparison to how we learn to apply Lean principles and practices.

Those of you who have had experience with both music and Lean should recognize the following:

Music	Lean
Requires development of fine fine motor skills	Requires development of thinking skills.
Most people need a teacher to learn music.	Most people need a sensei to learn Lean.
Can't play music if you can't remember the notes.	Can't do Lean if you can't remember the principles.
Must practice every day.	Must practice every day.
Requires a great deal of personal motivation and discipline.	Requires a great deal of personal motivation and discipline.
Follows strict rules for timing, sequence, and synchronization with other people (instruments).	Follows strict rules for timing, sequence, and synchronization with other people (departments).
Can't just play music (do). Musician must think and do.	Lean requires people to think and do (most people just do without thinking).
Errors are broken down into minute parts, investigated thoroughly, and corrected.	Problems are broken down into minute parts, investigated thoroughly, and corrected.

Typically a small group activity, and requires real teamwork.	Typically a small group activity, and requires real teamwork.
Establish the basic chords and fingering, then work out the problems one-by-one over time.	Establish the process, then work out remaining problems one-by-one over time.
Must adhere to standard work (sheet music).	Must adhere to standard work (combination sheet).
Must know both your part (the detail) and the whole song (broad view).	Must know both your part (the detail) and the whole process (broad view).
Symbols and notation have precise meaning.	Symbols and notation have precise meaning.
Music has rules.	Lean management has rules.
Players must play just-in-time.	Material and information must be just-in-time.
Learn music mostly by doing.	Learn Lean management mostly by doing.
Sees overproduction, movement, defects, waiting, and transportation as waste.	Recognize existence of 7 wastes + 1 (behavioral).
You're never done; always more to learn.	You're never done; always more to learn.

Further, think of music notes organized and processed as batch-and-queue compared to Lean. Batch-and-queue music looks like this (bass clef, standard and TAB notation, 4/4 time):

What does it sound like?
Go to: www.theclbm.com/reallean1.html to listen.

Few people would listen to batch-and-queue music. They'd find the repetition of a single note and long waits terribly boring and likely annoying. Batch-and-queue manufacturing and service businesses are also boring and annoying to employees, customers, suppliers, etc.

Lean music looks like this (bass clef, standard and TAB notation, 4/4 time):

What does it sound like?
Go to: www.theclbm.com/reallean1.html to listen [1].

Lean music is what we enjoy listening to. Lean businesses are also more vibrant and appealing to associates, customers, suppliers, etc., which of course leads to better results for investors.

Most people are capable of learning how to play a musical instrument to a fairly high degree of proficiency – at least enough to play at a level that is personally satisfying. However, only a few people are motivated to teach themselves how to play music well.

Most people hire a teacher whose role is not only to teach music but to impose discipline for practicing upon the student. The same thing happens when we hire a sensei to teach us Lean. However, most music students usually lose interest, which is why teachers encounter only a few dedicated students over their entire teaching career. That is also what sensei experience.

This should lead us to think more deeply about who is better suited to lead the Lean transformation. Perhaps not just any President or CEO will do. It seems to take one who is willing to learn, be comfortable as a beginner, and practice relentlessly every day for years and years. It's a lot like learning how to play the guitar. Skill and understanding can only develop with practice.

But unfortunately, most people don't practice often enough or just stop practicing because music, like Lean, is harder than it looks and there is much more to it than we initially think. Failing to persevere has a cost: it compromises the boss' ability to teach and lead.

On the other hand, if you continue practicing you become proficient. That is what the people of Toyota Motor Corporation have done. As a result, they now operate at a level comparable to a superior classical music composer and multi-instrumentalist performance artist, having continuously developed and improved their capabilities over seven decades.

What Toyota people have accomplished thus far is impressive, and even more so as details emerge that describe how top managers think and what they do (see the books listed under "Further Reading").

Grounded in reality, practical, committed to business principles and corporate purpose, thorough, consistent, dedicated, and disciplined, they are akin to a master musician – yet still striving to learn, which yields better capabilities to teach and leaders with credibility.

Toyota has become the Bach of management [2].

Notes

[1] Audioslave, "Your Time Has Come," *Out of Exile*, Interscope Records, 2005.

[2] Johann Sebastian Bach, 1685-1750. See http://www.jsbach.org/biography.html. Why did I pick Bach instead of, say, Mozart? After all, "the Mozart of management" sounds much better. The reasons are: 1) Bach was a small town guy, like the Toyoda family once were; 2) Bach was a hands-on man - he made his living in part as an organ mechanic; 3) Bach's work was not recognized in his lifetime, same as for Kiichiro Toyoda; and 4) Bach was left-handed. The Lean management system has characteristics of left-handedness, such as counter-clockwise flow in cells, Ohno's "thinking in reverse," pull systems, etc.

Further Reading

- S. Kamiya, *My Life With Toyota*, Toyota Motor Sales Co., Ltd., Japan, 1976

- Y. Sugimori, K. Kusunoki, F. Cho, and S. Uchikawa, "Toyota Production System and Kanban System – Materialization of Just-in-Time and Respect-for-Human System," *International Journal of Production Research*, Vol. 15, No. 6, pp. 553-564, 1977

- S. Shingo, *Study of 'Toyota' Production System from Industrial Engineering Viewpoint, Japan Management Association*, Tokyo, Japan, November (distributed by Productivity Press, Inc., Cambridge , MA), 1981

- S. Kato, *My Years with Toyota*, Toyota Motor Sales Co., Ltd., Japan, 1981

- E. Toyoda, Toyota: *Fifty Years in Motion*, Kodansha International, New York, NY, 1985

- T. Ohno, *Toyota Production System*, Productivity Press, Portland, OR, 1988

- *Toyota: A History of the First 50 Years*, Toyota Motor Corporation, Toyota City (Nagoya), Japan, 1988

- S. Kimoto, *Quest for the Dawn*, The Dougherty Company, Milwaukee, WI, 1991

- Y. Togo and W. Wartman, *Against All Odds: The Story of Toyota Motor Corporation and The Family That Created It*, St. Martin's Press, New York, NY, 1993

- Y. Monden, *Toyota Production System: An Integrated Approach to Just-*

In-Time, Engineering and Management Press, Norcross, GA, 1998

- A. Kawahara, *The Origin of Competitive Strength*, Springer-Verlag, Tokyo, Japan, 1998
- Y. Togo, *Yuki Togo's Sell Like Hell!!*, self-published, 1998
- T. Fujimoto, *The Evolution of a Manufacturing System at Toyota*, Oxford University Press, New York, NY, 1999
- S. Basu, *Corporate Purpose: Why It Matters More than Strategy*, Garland Publishing, Inc. New York, NY, 1999
- Toyota Motor Corporation, "The Toyota Way 2001," internal document, Toyota City (Nagoya), Japan, April 2001
- S. Hino, *Inside the Mind of Toyota*, Productivity Press, New York, NY, 2006

7 Remembering What Ohno and Shingo Said

*Ohno, the creator of the Toyota Production System, and
Shingo, a contributor to TPS, had a lot of concern that
people might misunderstand it. Here's a reminder
of some key points they made.*

While the foundation of Toyota Production System (TPS) was laid by Sakichi Toyoda (jidoka) and his son Kiichiro (Just-in-Time), Taiichi Ohno, who rose to the level of Executive Vice President of Toyota Motor Corporation, is widely credited with making TPS a reality. Shigeo Shingo, a consultant to Toyota, famous for his work on single-minute exchange of dies (SMED), was an important contributor of basic industrial engineering practice. Eiji Toyoda, former President of Toyota Motor Corporation, and Saito Naichi also played key roles [1]. And let's not forget the many nameless team members whose efforts also helped make TPS come alive.

Mr. Ohno wrote a book titled: *Toyota Production System* in 1978. The book was translated into English and published by Productivity Press in 1988 [2]. The focus of Ohno's book was to describe the thinking behind TPS, at a high level and with very few specific examples, and primarily intended for an audience of senior managers.

Mr. Shingo wrote a book titled: *A Study of 'Toyota' Production System from Industrial Engineering Viewpoint*, 1980 [3]. Shingo's intended his book to compliment Ohno's book, but with greater focus on the method of implementation and for an audience of mid-managers and professional workers such as industrial engineers [4].

Shingo's book was translated into English by the Japan Management Association and distributed by Productivity Press in 1981. The English translation had poor grammar and contained many spelling errors. Norman Bodek, then the president of Productivity Press Inc., obtained rights to revise the English translation [5] which he published in 1989 [6]. Despite its shortcomings, the original translation is a valuable resource for understanding many important details about the Toyota Production System.

These two books are essential reading for anyone who is serious about understanding TPS [7]. Purchase them both and read them again and again, from different perspectives.

Both Ohno and Shingo were very concerned that people would misunderstand TPS. So in their respective books, they tried to make sure that readers would come away with an accurate understanding of TPS. So it is with this in mind that the following selected passages are presented, followed by some commentary to interpret and amplify its meaning.

Ohno's Words [2]

> "The Toyota production system, however, is not just a production system. I am confident it will reveal its strength as a management system..." (p. xv)

Commentary: Ohno is saying: don't take the word "production" literally. However, that is exactly what most people have done, and thus they think of TPS as just a "manufacturing thing." To Ohno, TPS is a management system for the entire organization, not solely the production part of the business. It can work in any business, because TPS is a principle-based management system. Comprehend your situation and apply the principles, as well as the associated tools and methods.

> "We kept reminding ourselves, however, that careless imitation of the American system [of production] could be dangerous." (p. 1)

Commentary: Likewise, we should remind ourselves that careless imitation of TPS is dangerous.

> "The basis of the Toyota production system is the absolute elimination of waste." (p. 4)

Commentary: For many managers, the basis for implementing TPS is to improve operating efficiency and increase the stock price. Most managers who think this way achieve little success with either operating efficiency or stock price. Ohno sees it the other way around: eliminating waste lowers costs, and what follows from that is improved profitability and higher stock price. Remember, people are not waste.

"...the workers themselves should push the stop button to halt production if any abnormality appears." (p. 7)

Commentary: While the context is stopping a machine in a production environment when a problem occurs, these same words surely apply to administrative processes as well.

"Although young and eager to push, I decided not to press for quick, drastic changes, but to be patient." (p. 11)

Commentary: Managers usually turn to TPS when a crisis emerges and will naturally lack patience for many things – including people's resistance to change. Being patient does not mean you won't quickly get where you want to be. Being impatient means you may never head in the direction you want to go.

"We must understand these situations in-depth before we can achieve a revolution in consciousness." (p. 15)

Commentary: The causes of overproduction, defects, etc., must be thoroughly understood by managers. Doing so will enable you to clearly see things that you were previously unable to see.

"...the Toyota production system has been built on the practice and evolution of this scientific approach [5 why's method of root cause analysis]." (p. 17)

Commentary: It seems many managers disdain the application of scientific methods in business – especially for management (vs. production or engineering) problems. They may think: "Who has time for science? We're running a business!" Just look at Toyota and see what can happen when you apply scientific methods to identify and understand a problem, apply countermeasures, and then test the countermeasures to determine if they eliminate the problem from recurring.

> "The Toyota production system clearly reveals excess manpower. Because of this, some…people have been suspicious of it as a means of laying off workers. But that is not the idea. Management's responsibility is to identify excess manpower and utilize it effectively." (p. 20)

Commentary: Managers who lay people off as a result of continuous improvement make a grave error because it undercuts worker participation in future improvement activities. Who would want to participate in continuous improvement activities if it may cost them their job? Since layoffs resulting from continuous improvement are commonplace, this helps explain why most companies have little success with Lean. Instead, managers must re-deploy excess workers to other value-creating activities. Remember, the literal definition of "kaizen." It means: "change for the better," in a multilateral context.

> "…the most important point in common between sports and work is the continuing need for practice and training. It is east to understand theory with the mind; the problem is to remember it with the body. The goal is to

know and do instinctively. Having the spirit to endure the training is the first step on the road to winning." (p. 25)

Commentary: Ohno is comparing TPS to sports – a human activity which requires an immense amount of practice if one is to successfully compete at the highest levels. To be good at TPS – as an associate, supervisor, or manager – you must practice it daily in order to "know and do instinctively." Do company executives have the spirit to endure the training? Do they view two days of TPS lessons in the classroom as training? Or, do they view regular participation in shop floor and office kaizen as the training?

"We use the computer freely, as a tool, and try not to be pushed around by it. But we reject the dehumanization caused by computers and the way they can lead to higher costs… we want information only when we need it… An industrial mind must be very realistic… (p. 48). In business, excess information must be suppressed." (p. 50)

Commentary: Computer systems are a tool that can be easily misused. We should not be ruled by them because we might start to think people are not needed to run the business. Only people can identify and eliminate waste. Computer systems are expensive in at least three ways: acquisition and maintenance costs; belief that all the information is accurate and useful for running a business; and people become distracted by useless data and excess information and thus fail to move TPS forward.

"I urge all managers, intermediate supervisors, fore-
men, and workers in production to be more flexible in
their thinking as they go about their work." (p. 115)

Commentary: Ohno is urging people to be more creative and
open to new ideas as they perform their respective activities.
Don't limit this great advice to production personnel. Flexible
thinking also means managers must move beyond the numbers to run a business, and do a better job incorporating non-
quantitative data in decision-making. In TPS, the reasons to
take action often can not be expressed in a spreadsheet.
Instead, you have to go to the place where the work is per-
formed and see for yourself.

Now let's review some of the things Mr. Shingo had to say.

Shingo's Words [3]

"... Toyota production system is the production system,
and kanban system is nothing but the means of carrying
out the production system and only a controlling system. Because kanban system has come up as a big merit
of Toyota production system, even in Japan, there is
misunderstanding that Toyota production system is
kanban system, and only the external phase [just the
part that people could see] was initiated, resulting in
failure or having little effect in many cases." (Preface,
p. 14)

Commentary: People mistakenly think TPS is the same as
kanban system. It is not. Blindly imitating kanban system

without understanding the overall intent of TPS – both human and technical – will cause problems.

"(a) Process [is] the course through which material is changed to the product. The content consists of four phenomena: processing, inspection, transportation, and storage. (b) Operation [is] the course through which man and machine work upon the product. In Europe and America, the term 'operation' is used also for 'processing' in process, but in this book the term 'operation' will be defined to the case of (b)... Toyota production system is explained based on such recognition. Consequently, 'process' and 'operation' are not in parallel relation..." (Preface, pp. 16-17)

Commentary: In TPS, "process" and "operation" are different. This distinction, which Shingo explains in detail, must be thoroughly understood.

"If Toyota production system is reviewed from the standpoint of fundamental production control system, the system must be applicable to factories in any country, as a universal production control system, being adapted to the characteristics of each plant, and I believe that big results could be expected. I sincerely hope that the enterprises in each country would recognize the essence and apply the system effectively by considering the characteristics of their own plant, without being misled by the external phase only." (Preface, p. 18)

Commentary: TPS is not simply a production system for the automotive industry. It can work in any factory – and now we know service enterprise as well – with adaptations if needed. Shingo advises caution: do not be misled by external appearances, because they do not inform you of the true intent of TPS.

"Regarding the abovesaid points [clarifications of what is meant by waste caused by overproduction, operation ratio of machine, and visible control] the plants which practices Toyota production system in its real sense and understand the fundamental idea can be all right, but those which only listened to the lecture or read the explanation and imitate simply are liable to fall into the abovesaid misunderstanding." (Preface, p. 24)

Commentary: TPS is learned mostly by doing, not by reading or listening to someone lecturing about it. Most organizations try to imitate TPS and do not truly understand it. As a result, many important aspects are misunderstood or not understood at all.

"...in order to implement plant improvements, it is quite important to understand the mechanism of production functions correctly. Misunderstanding of the fundamentals might not always lead to effective improvements. Therefore cautions must be necessary for this point." (p. 6)

Commentary: To most people, addressing the symptom of a problem and not its root cause(s) is acceptable evidence of improvement. Shingo says we must first understand production activities as a network of processes and operations in order to achieve effective improvements.

"Therefore, this SMED system is one of the fundamental method that had an important meaning for the development of Toyota production system." (p. 70)

Commentary: Without SMED (single minute exchange of dies), there is no TPS. The principles of SMED also apply to production activities in service businesses.

"Now you might think that Toyota Motor is wearing a smart suit, so you would intend to purchase one, and bought a suit called 'kanban system' but your body was bubbled-up so fat that you could not wear it. Therefore, it would be necessary to improve formation (improvement of production system). Besides, you must definitely understand the meaning of basic health (consideration to eliminate useless items thoroughly). This is the way I talk to people." (pp. 93-94)

Commentary: Shingo likes to give analogies to help people understand the true meaning and intent of TPS. Kanban system is not something you can simply buy and fit into your existing "fat" production system. You would first have to improve the health of your production system by eliminating waste.

"It is stated that one of the great mainstays of Toyota production system is 'Just in Time.' But, if the language should be translated into Japanese it would be 'timely or well timed....' 'Just in Time' involves the meaning that each process must be supplied with required items, at the required time and in the required quantity... This thinking is the proper understanding." (pp. 98-99)

Commentary: Shingo is concerned that people take the meaning of Just-in-Time literally, so that the only aspect they are concerned about is time. Of course, people must supply processes at the required time, but they must also be concerned about supplying the process with the required items in the required quantity – and to the required location.

> "When you get appendicitis, relieve the pain by ice-cooling it from the outside. This method is useless, so Toyota production system proceeds thus: Treat appendicitis by operation and cut-off the affected part. Therefore, appendicitis would never recur life-time. Namely, execute basical solutions to prevent recurrence... When troubles occur, grab the actual cause even stopping the line and prevent repeated recurrence for the future." (pp. 107,109)

Commentary: It is useless to treat the symptom of problems. So when problems occur, understand the root cause and apply countermeasures that completely prevent recurrence. Recognizing a problem and understanding its actual causes is so important to the proper functioning of TPS that it is OK to stop the work.

> "...but does [MRP] involve the followings of the Toyota production system?
> • Remarkable shortening of time for exchange of dies and toolings
> • Through that reduction of time, accomplish small lot production
> • Perform one piece flow operation consistently from parts processing to the assembly process

- Considering order production and adopt the method of receiving products from latter processes

It is doubtful whether that system [MRP] deeply considers the improvements of the fundamental points of the control system itself." (pp. 296-297)

Commentary: Shingo is questioning if material requirements planning (MRP) software systems support or contradict TPS. Shingo concludes – in 1981 – that MRP is inconsistent with TPS because it does not support single minute exchange of dies, small lot production, one-piece flow, and pull systems – and continuous improvement of these elements of production control.

"But, the thing which is most important and requiring time is as follows: The top managements must have a clear understanding and earnest will to achieve the final aim, and besides, the most important point is to have the entire plant realize and understand, especially, realization and understanding of the people at the production site must be obtained. This is the key point that would lead to success or failure." (p. 333)

Commentary: Senior managers must understand TPS thoroughly, which can only be achieved through direct participation. It is their responsibility to inform workers about TPS so they realize and understand the purpose of what they are doing and why it needs to be done. Not doing so will lead to failure.

In closing, these two great books contain essential insights into he correct understanding and application of Toyota production system that serious students of TPS will enjoy reading over and over again – in support of actual doing.

Notes

[1] T. Ohno with S. Mito, *Just-In-Time For Today and Tomorrow*, Productivity Press, Cambridge, MA, 1988, p. 75

[2] T. Ohno, *Toyota Production System*, Productivity Press, Portland, OR, 1988

[3] S. Shingo, *Study of 'Toyota' Production System from Industrial Engineering Viewpoint*, Japan Management Association, Tokyo, Japan, November 1981, distributed by Productivity Press, Inc., Cambridge, MA

[4] For more details, see Y. Monden, *Toyota Production System: An Integrated Approach to Just-In-Time*, Engineering and Management Press, Norcross, GA, 1998

[5] N. Bodek, *Kaikaku: The Power and Magic of Lean*, PCS Press, Vancouver, WA, pp. 63-65, 67-68, 147, and 188

[6] S. Shingo, *A Study of the Toyota Production System*, Productivity Press, Inc., Portland, OR, 1989

[7] The original 1981 English translation of Shingo's book can be purchased online through used bookers such as alibris.com, barnesandnoble.com, or amazon.com.

8 Myth-Busting Using Value Stream Maps

*Current state value stream maps reveal much more than
just material and information flows. They also inform
us of the gaps that often exist between what top managers
say and what is actually happening in the workplace.*

The value stream map is one of many ways that Lean-minded people organize data to yield accurate information about what is going on in order to initiate actions to improve a process [1]. While we should not over-emphasize value stream maps [2] – they are not the beginning and end of Lean – they do provide a lot of useful information. However, they can also provide important information beyond our current understanding of material and information flows.

Within the last three years, the use of value stream maps has been expanded to include:

- Determining value stream profit and loss [3]
- Calculating the amount of greenhouse gas produced by a value stream [4]
- As a tool to diagnose and correct deficiencies in leadership performance [5]

It turns out that value stream maps are useful in other ways. Understanding the broader utility of value stream maps can help managers identify many other desirable improvements.

A fifth way value stream maps can be used is for corporate myth-busting. Simply looking at the current state value

stream map for a shop or office process can help us discern
the validity of what top managers say. For example:

What Many Managers Say	What Current State VSMs Reveal
"There is a shortage of qualified leaders."	Not possible. Anyone can create a wasteful current state.
"We are totally committed improvement."	No. Manager must have some other definition of improvement in mind.
"Teamwork is critical to our success."	In reality there is a lack of teamwork as evidenced by separately positioned processes and poor information flows.
"What gets measured gets managed."	No. Metrics currently in use do not help people improve processes or working conditions.
"Executive compensation is tied to performance."	Performance is poor, therefore executive pay should be low.
"Employees are our greatest asset."	Not if 80% or more of employee's time is wasted.
"We don't have the resources" or "We are stretched too thin."	There are an abundance of resources waiting to be deployed effectively.
"There is a shortage of skilled workers" or "Business is complex."	No. Managers have not led efforts to simplify and create standard work.
"We are in a mature market."	It is more likely customers

	are dissatisfied with your performance and also want things you don't offer.
"Greater scale makes us more competitive" or "Higher volume will lower our costs."	Eliminating waste, unevenness, and unreasonableness lowers costs and improves competitiveness.
"We can't compete against China."	Waste, unevenness, and unreasonableness is hurting your ability to compete against anyone.
"We listen to what our employees say."	Improvement suggestions from workers have long been ignored.
"Innovation is the key to our success."	Production process innovation is clearly absent. New product or service processes are probably not too good either.
"We are acting with a tremendous sense of urgency."	You are doing the same wasteful things faster.
"We treat our employees with dignity and respect."	Actually, you're wasting their lives by having them do activities that add cost but do not add value.
"Everyone is working very hard."	Yes, people do look busy, but that doesn't mean they are doing any value-added work.
"We must execute flawlessly" and "Failure is not an option."	There will be many flaws, and failure is certain at some point.

As you can see, current state value stream maps are a Rosetta Stone for deciphering today's management-speak. Can you think of others?

While the true condition of an organization may not be very pretty, it is important to understand things as they actually are because this is the starting point for meaningful improvement.

Hopefully, this will inspire managers to further improve themselves and their areas of responsibility. But how? They can start by dedicating themselves to learn and practice what they were probably not taught to do in college or graduate school:

- Observe processes
- Identify problems and gather data
- Determine root causes (e.g. 5 Why's, fishbone diagram)
- Identify countermeasures [6], and
- Regularly participate in activities to simplify processes and eliminate waste, unevenness, and unreasonableness.

Please remember to also practice non-blaming and non-judgmental behaviors, as these are required for realizing genuine continuous improvement [7,8].

Notes

[1] M. Rother and J. Shook, *Learning to See*, v. 1.3, Lean Enterprise Institute, Brookline, MA, 2003

[2] A. Smalley, "TPS vs. Lean and the Law of Unintended Consequences", Superfactory.com, Jan 2006, http://www.superfactory.com/articles/smalley_tps_vs_lean.htm

[3] B. Maskell and B. Baggaley, *Practical Lean Accounting*, Productivity Press, New York, NY, 2003

[4] D. Simons and R. Mason, "Lean and Green: Doing More with Less," *ECR Journal*, Vol. 3, No. 1, Spring 2003, pp. 84-91

[5] M.L. Emiliani and D.J. Stec, "Using Value Stream Maps to Improve Leadership," *Leadership and Organizational Development Journal*, Vol. 25, No. 8, pp. 622-645, 2004

[6] S. Spear, "Learning to Lead at Toyota," *Harvard Business Review*, Vol. 82, No. 5, 2004, pp. 78-86

[7] M. Imai, "Kaizen Seminar", Hartford Graduate Center, Hartford, Conn., May 1988

[8] Toyota Motor Corporation, "The Toyota Way 2001," internal document, Toyota City, Japan, April 2001

9 The Tragedy of Waste

As is often the case, great ideas and practices are the result of many people's thoughts and labors over many years. Things that seem new to us were often known by others long ago. Taking a look back in time to how people understood the meaning of waste in industrial management can help us understand present-day challenges.

The Tragedy of Waste is the title of a long-forgotten book written by Mr. Stuart Chase (1888-1985) and published in 1925 [1]. I came across this book as I was researching industrial management and engineering texts published between 1910 and 1930. The title alone was very intriguing, given the prominence of waste in Lean management. More importantly, it turns out the contents of the book had much to reveal about what people at that time understood about waste and how to eliminate it.

Stuart Chase was an accountant interested in improving the efficiency and economic performance of government and industry [2]. He was a prolific author, having written more than a dozen books. *The Tragedy of Waste* gained world-wide attention [3] for the direct way in which it exposed big problems in industrial planning, production, and consumption.

The English language version of the book almost certainly found its way to Japan (Hokkaido University library has a copy, for example). It is not known if *The Tragedy of Waste* was translated into Japanese or if it influenced the thinking of

Kiichiro Toyoda, Eiji Toyoda, or Taiichi Ohno. We do know that Henry Ford's book, *Today and Tomorrow*, published in 1926 [4], discussed waste at length and did influence Ohno's thinking [5].

It is likely that Henry Ford read Chase's book, as well a 1921 book titled *Waste in Industry* [6], written by a committee of engineers chaired by Herbert Hoover (whose undergraduate degree was in geology). Hoover, a Republican, became the 31st President of the United States (1929-1933), and was perhaps the only President who had a good understanding of waste [7]. Some of the facts, figures, and sources and causes of waste found in *Waste in Industry* appeared in Chase's book.

The New York Times had this to say about *The Tragedy of Waste*:

> "An exciting and informing book. The author has surveyed this sorry world and has shown how absurdly it is organized and managed. That one-half of productive man-power is waste is the conclusion at which he has arrived." [8]

It was worth reading then, and again now, because it informs us of the rich history of modern industrial management and the people who long ago dedicated their lives to eliminating waste and improving the workplace and economic standing of the country and its citizens.

The Tragedy of Waste was written in an era of enlightenment when it came to the application modern industrial management practices. Frederick Winslow Taylor (1856-1915) and his colleagues Frank and Lillian Gilbreth were key figures in the "Progressive Era" [9], which advocated improving efficiency through the application of scientific methods. Taylor's 1911 book, *The Principles of Scientific Management* [10] became an early work on a body of knowledge what would soon be known as "industrial engineering."

The development of Scientific Management and evolution into industrial engineering in the United States in the late-1800's and early-1900's links directly to the U.S. government's World War II-era "Training Within Industry" program. This program was exported to Japan at the conclusion of World War II to aid in re-building Japan's industrial base, and forms the roots of kaizen as practiced by Toyota Motor Corporation personnel [11]. In addition, Shigeo Shingo's "P-Course," taught at Toyota from 1955-1980 [12], was derived in part from these early industrial engineering works.

It is interesting to note the Progressive Era was very much intertwined with politics and political thinking of the day. At the time, opponents of the Progressives generally characterized them as left-leaning; liberal, socialist, or even communist depending upon the commentator [2]. I'll return to that point later.

So what did Chase have to say about waste? The starting point is the onset of the World War in April 1917. Chase discusses at length how 25% of the workforce was displaced from their civilian jobs to fight in the war within several months. Did the productive output of the nation decline? No it did not; in fact, it increased. The remaining civilian workforce produced as much goods as when there were 25% more workers. Was this a miracle? Mr. Chase states:

> "No miracle. Only common sense. Faced with grave national danger, and acting under the psychological unity which common danger imparts to a group, the warring nations re-organized their industrial systems on the principle that a straight line is the shortest distance between two points. This principle tends to become mislaid in times of peace. It is not operating now in 1925 for instance." (pp. 7-8)

Isn't it interesting how the managers in the few companies that have done Lean well for many years do not lose their business sense of "danger" – the competition. Amazingly, for over eight decades, Toyota management has not lost its sense of crisis [13] nor has it mislaid the straight line principle.

Chase goes on to say:

> "During the war, the sense of crisis created the unity necessary for control [of economic activity and resources by the U.S. government]." (p. 8)

> "War control lifted the economic system of the country, stupefied by decades of profit-seeking, and hammered it and pounded it into an intelligent mechanism for delivering goods and services according to the needs of the army and of the working population. Money tended to fall out of the picture… yet the standard of living for the underlying population [was raised]." (p. 10)

> "[After the war] reconstruction collapsed, normalcy

returned, output slumped drastically, unemployment raised its ugly head, 1921 registered a terrible business depression… with four men back on the job, the house went up more slowly than it had done with three. An economic system which can, by taking thought, make three men do the work of four, merits perhaps a rather careful examination into the sources and extent of economic waste." (p. 11)

In other words, Chase was asking why, when faced with a crisis, we respond in ways that are good for us: more efficient, more productive, and conserving of resources. But when peace comes, we return to our wasteful ways and the standard of living declines. Sound familiar?

Mr. Chase favored a *functional society*,

"…where industry is devoted primarily to supplying human wants, and where profits are a by-product." (p. 23)

In contrast, the current system, Chase said, is less desirable:

"…*acquisitive society*, where property is a right anterior to, and independent of function; and where accordingly, production to meet necessary requirements becomes a by-product rather than the main end of economic activity." (p. 23).

In other words, producing useful goods and services are simply by-products of profit-seeking in an acquisitive society. Chase goes on to say:

"Our standard for measuring waste must in the end be based squarely on a functional conception of industry." (p. 24)

Thus, Chase disliked luxury goods and services sought by the wealthy. His focus was the practical needs and necessities of people, as well as improving the human condition by eliminating malnutrition, reducing infant mortality, better housing, eliminating illiteracy and ignorance, etc.

Chase, the accountant, had close ties to engineers and liked the way they thought about and analyzed problems. He preferred to use "the engineer's definition" of waste:

"...any bar to maximum use value of output at minimum real cost in energy and materials." (p. 16)

Today's definition of waste in the context of Lean management is [14]:

"Any activity that consumes resources but creates no value for the customer."

Chase thought of industrial output in two parts: the actual amount of goods and services required, and the effectiveness of the methods used to produce the requirements. He describes "four main channels of waste" (pp. 30-37):

- Wastes in Consumption
- Idle Man-Power
- Wastes in the Technique of Production and Distribution
- The Waste of Natural Resources

Chase did not to assign blame for all the waste in industry, saying: "There is no occasion for blame or recrimination." (p. 28).

1. Wastes in Consumption

Chase defines this as: "…the production of goods which lie outside the category of human wants." (p. 30). This includes "the perversion of wants and harmful products," goods made prior to the production of sufficient quantities of the necessities, or goods that should have never been produced.

Chase went on to say:

> "If somehow the consumer could be educated to demand the things which tend to give maximum value at minimum cost, a great amount of productive labor might be saved." (p. 32)

2. Idle Man-Power

Chase defines this as unemployment due to seasonal variations in production, business depressions, and "residual unemployment," as well as losses due to changing jobs, labor strikes, preventable accidents and sickness, absenteeism, "lost labor of the idle rich," and "lost labor of the hobo and bum." (p. 33).

3. Wastes in the Technique of Production and Distribution

Chase defines this as: "Wastes in the techniques of distribution – excessive selling costs, duplication of wholesale and retail facilities, cross-hauling." (p. 36). He points out the vast improvements in output that are achieved simply by improving plant and equipment layout, and then asks to what extent could productivity be improved if production were located closer to the source of raw materials? He notes many cases in which raw materials and production are separated by great distances. For example, the raw materials for shoe manufacturing in New England are located in the Midwest, so it would make a lot more sense for shoe manufacturing to be located in the Midwest.

4. The Waste of Natural Resources

Chase defines this as: "…the destruction of natural resources, over and above the needs of prudent current consumption." (p. 36). In this section, he describes how waste should be measured. He says it should not be measured in dollars because of the changing value of money over time. Instead, waste should be measured in "…man-power or raw materials by physical count [i.e. physical units of measure such as pounds, feet, etc.]…" (p. 38). This is partly how we measure waste today.

Mr. Chase criticizes many things due to the waste associated with them, including: conspicuous consumption among the leisure class, excessive product variety, illicit drugs, proliferation of "patent drugs," adulteration and poor quality of raw materials, trade industry associations, quackery and get-rich-quick-schemes, speculation and gambling, luxuries and super-luxuries, fashions, secret processes and formulas which lead to duplication of effort, and drinks with alcohol content over 10%. Tobacco, like alcohol, is a "legitimate want," provided it does not become "unduly inflated by the appeals of advertisers." (p. 68).

Chase also criticizes the "overhead professions" and their job growth – what we would today call service industry occupations. He notes the legitimate need for them, but questions the number of positions they occupy compared to the value-adding occupations. For example, the insurance business, while necessary and useful to an extent,

> "… creates nothing. It simply keeps busy a few hundred thousand clerks, actuaries, salesmen, lawyers, printers… and passing pieces of paper from hand to hand…" (p. 103)

Chase is highly critical of advertising, devoting a whole chapter to it. He says:

> "Advertising… is the life blood of quackery… It is not an end product. No one consumes advertising directly. It is an intermediate service which points the to consumption and which enters into the cost of consumption…" (p. 107)

Chase does note a special case in which advertising could be useful:

> "National advertising, for the education of the consumer, if conducted by some impartial scientific body might conceivably provide a great channel for eliminating wastes in consumption." (p. 113)

Mr. Chase, along with F.J. Schlink, founded Consumers' Research in 1929, a nonprofit consumer advocate organization and a forerunner to Consumers Union which publishes *Consumer Reports*.

Later in the book, Chase notes:

> "The tendency of modern business seems to run in the
> direction of nullifying economies in production by
> throwing the gains into greater outlays for salesman-
> ship." (p. 212)

Of course, greater outlays in sales are only the tip of the ice-
berg. Today we also see improvement in shop and office
processes nullified by greater outlays in expenses for ever-
more management personnel, executive pay, top-tier management consulting firms, etc.

Chapter nine focuses on wastes in production, a familiar topic
to Lean people. Chase laments that industry has failed "to
take advantage of these demonstrated methods [of Scientific
Management], and shuffles along in its own rut in its own
way..." (p. 146). He cites mistakes and blunders made in the
application of Scientific Management, including:

> "The quacks, as in the case of every new discovery,
> descend in hordes and succeed as usual in discounting
> a good part of the value of the movement... In many
> cases, the 'extra high wages' to be paid [to laborers] for
> approaching performance standards turned out to be a
> carrot in front of the donkey's nose. The whole value of
> waste elimination was pocketed by the employer, leav-
> ing the worker no share beyond an increased deposit of
> fatigue poisons." (p. 149)

Chase notes that Scientific Management has widespread
applicability:

> "It may invade the home and time-study the labor of

washing dishes. It may study marketing and distribution methods... It is a universal technique, and anybody's to use who has the intelligence and perseverance to apply it to his own problem." (p. 153)

Standardization, of course, is a prominent feature in Scientific Management and later in industrial engineering practice. Poor production methods, poor management, and a lack of standardization in the boot and shoe business means:

"Here we have, not unemployment on the streets, but unemployment on the job – workers sitting around a third of their time waiting for materials to come along." (p. 155)

While the Progressives got many things right, they did get some important things wrong, such as small lot production.

"The 'sell the goods before you make them' policy is prevalent [in men's clothing], and, as in the case of the metal industry, is disastrous to internal shop efficiency. It forces manufacture in small lots... Small lots mean constant interruption in work and a high cost per garment." (p. 158)

When it came to product variation, the recommendation was to limit sizes and styles to enable large lot production:

"If the industry had foresight enough to study its records of actual sales, it could concentrate on these comparatively few sizes and styles and plan in advance for large lot production on a balanced load basis." (p. 158)

People have long misunderstood the meaning of the word "standardization." According to Chase:

> "The word 'standardization' is perhaps an unhappy one. It connotes in the lay reader's mind a dead level of uniformity, regimentation; an industrial goose step... A better name for it might be 'simplification'." (pp. 171-172)

Chase criticizes as wasteful the great number of businesses competing in the same market trying to sell too great a variety of products. He discusses industrial coordination spanning both inter- and intra-plant levels (and at national and global levels) as a means to improve the entire system, rather than optimizing individual parts. Chase speaks of this in a manner similar to how Womack and Jones have recently described Lean consumption [15].

> "Coordination means planning for a given end. It means the traffic cop instead of a free-for-all... it means the ascertaining of human requirements in bulk terms of food, shelter, clothing, and the adaptation of the productive plant and the distributive system to meet them with a minimum of lost motion." (pp. 176-177)

Chase talks about production load balancing, and points out the multiple errors and waste associated with building plant capacity for peak load versus average load:

> "February and August are the 'peak load' months, and they determine the capacity of the shop. You must accordingly have over three times three times as large a shop, and three times as much machinery, to make 9000

pairs of shoes on a *peak load* basis, as you would require on a *balanced load* basis of a steady 30 pairs per day." (p. 185)

He also talks of customers batching their orders which contributed to idleness of equipment and workers during non-peak periods. He says further:

"Peak loads are not always cyclical or seasonal. They may occur weekly or daily... the Meat Packing industry shows Monday and Wednesday peaks in the run of animals over the killing beds. Slaughtering plants must be designed to handle these peaks. On other days of the week, much of the capacity is idle." (pp. 187-188)

Thus, we see that Chase and his contemporaries understood the problems caused by unevenness (mura, in Japanese).

Chase is concerned about how to address the wasteful human tendency among top managers to intentionally restrict output in order to raise prices.

"One wonders what the Scientific Management engineers can do when they collide with this principle. Their work in such an event can only be a saving at the spigot while the bunghole runs.... The true engineer wants to see the shop running at approximately full capacity every working day – maximum output, minimum effort. The true business man with his eye on his sales sheet, cannot afford to think of the shop in such terms. If more money is to be made by going on half-time, then he must go on half-time. And it is the business man and not the engineer who has the final word." (p. 191)

Chase is concerned about the waste in distribution because "There is a gathering opinion in the United States that it costs more to distribute things than it does to produce them." (p. 209). He notes that in 1850 there were one distributor for every four producers, but by 1920 there was one distributor for each producer. The rising numbers of distributors add cost but do not create value.

> "It costs 19 cents to make a Gillette safety razor for which you pay five dollars. The profit will not reach one dollar, leaving a 'distribution' cost, including selling and advertising, of at least $3.80 as against the factory cost of 19 cents." (p. 213)

Along with this, Chase notes how orders for perishable goods are forced into the market and distributed in advance of known requirements, resulting in spoilage and higher costs to the consumer. High-pressure sales persons and company sales policies, such as "new brands and new systems of rebates" (p. 217) and channel stuffing are cited as contributing factors. He notes that each company in the chain of producers and suppliers is doing this – i.e. point optimization. Thus, advertising, sales, and distribution constitute an enormous amount of waste and added cost.

There is also the problem of too many suppliers serving too few customers:

> "In the Rochester Milk Survey of 1912, it was found that

the milk wagons in use traveled a combined total of 447 miles a day, where a unified delivery system would have required only 39.1 miles – or 9% of the competitive total. In one section, 273 homes were supplied by 27 distributors traveling 25 miles, whereas one dealer could render the same service traveling not more than 2.6 miles. The survey concluded with the statement that the City of Rochester under a unified system of milk distribution could be served at one-third the current cost, saving consumers a half a million dollars, or a possible reduction in price of about 2 cents a quart." (p. 224)

The chapter on natural resources gives a detailed description of the large amount of waste in the production and utilization of basic commodities such as water, minerals, oil, coal, natural gas, and lumber.

Overall, Chase finds the total amount of waste in industry is 30-50% (p. 207). This means that output could be doubled within existing resources, for the purpose of improving the human condition by making available to all citizens the necessities of life at low cost. In addition,

"Waste elimination does not call for a hard, bright, regimented efficiency… It calls for a life more abundant – for living instead of existing." (p. 276)

Yes, we should enjoy the fruits our labors.

The final chapter is called "The Challenge of Waste." Chase tackled the question of how to get people to recognize and respond to waste – a question dear to all our hearts. Chase

notes that "The engineering aspect is probably manageable."
(p. 277). But,

> "The point at issue is the behavior of the animal
> [man]... social psychology as a science is still in
> embryo... The way out turns on a genuine science of
> social psychology more than it turns on any other sin-
> gle factor." (p. 278)

Chase clearly favored the type of business man who had a
balanced view of the human and economic nature of business,
and spoke of the growing divide between them and the type
of business man more narrowly focused on the economic
aspects of business:

> "And we note the gathering cleavage between stock-
> and-bond business men like Mr. [Elbert] Gary and
> engineer business men like Mr. [Henry] Ford. Mr. Gary
> [co-founder of U.S. Steel] sees industry primarily in
> terms of profitable investment, while Mr. Ford sees it as
> primarily in terms of services turned out on a balanced
> load basis – with still an eye to his own profit and loss
> account." (pp. 278-279)

> "In short, it is by no means clear that the engineering
> type of business man will not ultimately supersede the
> stock-and-bond type, and so usher in a functional soci-
> ety of sorts while the radicals are still baying for the
> abolition of the profit system." (p. 279).

> "So far as we see the future of the abatement of waste
> it lies with the man of science – the social scientist,

the engineer." (p. 279)

Perhaps this is too tight a focus. After all, "...it is the business man and not the engineers who has the final word." (p. 191). The abatement of waste – and unevenness and unreasonableness – lie with all business men and women who can reason, who are willing to learn, and who will invest their labor into improvement.

Chase thought the abatement of waste "...lies with the man of science – the social scientist, the engineer." The type of influential social scientist he wanted was the psychologist to determine what would motivate people to act. But the influential social scientist he got instead was the economist who, it turns out, created theories – many filled with assumptions that result in ideal, non-real world conditions but help facilitate mathematical modeling [17, 18] – which did in fact motivate people to act, but in ways that led to increases in waste through widespread point optimization in free markets.

Lastly, I return the negative left-leaning political characterization given to Progressives by their opponents. Could this image or some remnant of it still exist? If so, it is interesting to speculate that this could be an important reason why many top managers of large corporations today, and in the past, have not fully adopted Lean management [16].

Perhaps Lean management simply does not line up with top management's politics. Perhaps it does not line up with the standard economic model most managers have in mind – that people are rational self-interested maximizers (i.e. point optimizers). Maybe Lean just smells wrong to them, for reasons they might not even be able to explain.

What we do know for certain is that most top managers adopt or create narrow derivative forms of Lean. Perhaps they do this because it provides a better fit to their own or society's mainstream political and economic views of business, inclusive of contemporary models of employee relations, corporate purpose and corporate governance. In their eyes, using a derivative form of Lean reduces the many risks that inevitably come with being different.

So the point of optimization is to be different, but not too different – but which leaves the best opportunities to eliminate waste, unevenness, and unreasonableness wholly unaddressed for many years.

Notes

[1] S. Chase, *The Tragedy of Waste*, The Macmillan Company, New York, NY, 1925. You can buy a used copy of this book from alibris.com or bn.com

[2] For more information on Stuart Chase, see http://aaahq.org/northeast/1999/p21.pdf by Richard Vangermeersch, http://en.wikipedia.org/wiki/ Stuart_Chase. Also see *The Life and Writings of Stuart Chase* (1888-1985), by Richard Vangermeersch, http://www.amazon.com/Life-Writings-Stuart-Chase-1888-1985/dp/0762312130/ref=sr_11_1/104-8197456-9027942?ie=UTF8

[3] W. Hodson, and J. Carfora, "Stuart Chase," *Harvard Magazine,* September-October 2004, p. 38 http://www.harvardmagazine.com/on-line/090431.html

[4] H. Ford, *Today and Tomorrow*, Doubleday, Page & Company, New York, NY., 1926

[5] T. Ohno, *Toyota Production System*, Productivity Press, Portland, OR, 1988, Chapter 5.

[6] *Waste in Industry*, By the Committee on Elimination of Waste in Industry of the Federated American Engineering Societies, Federated American Engineering Societies, Washington, D.C., distributed by McGraw-Hill Book Company, Inc., New York, NY, 1921. The first sentence of the Introduction says: "In making the studies upon which this report is based and in preparing the report itself there has been no purpose or desire to place blame on any individual, group or class." (p. 3). The final paragraph of the Introduction says: "…before there can be a material reduction in the sum total of waste in industry, much earnest, painstaking work must be done. The solution of such a problem is not one of hours or days but of years. Fundamental changes in our economic, financial, managerial and operating concepts and practices will be required. There will be need of both cooperative and individual effort. As regards groups, each must frankly face its own responsibility and meet its own duties. Each individual – plant executive or worker – must discover his own opportunities and then accept responsibility for performance." (pp. 6-7). The four aspects of waste in industry cited are: "1. Low production caused by faulty management of materials, plant, equipment, and men. 2. Interrupted production, caused by idle men, idle materials, idle plants, idle equipment. 3. Restricted production intentionally caused by owners, management, or labor. 4. Lost production caused by ill health, physical defects and industrial accidents." (p. 8). The first paragraph in Chapter II says: "Management has the greatest opportunity and hence responsibility for eliminating waste in industry. The opportunity and responsibility of labor is no less real though smaller in degree." (p. 8).

[7] For more information on President Hoover, see http://hoover.archives.gov/ and http://en.wikipedia.org/wiki/Herbert_Hoover

[8] From back cover of the dust jacket, 1929 edition, published by Grosset and Dunlap. The back cover contains an image of money slipping out of one's hands, while the front cover contains a menacing image of a hooded grim reaper, hand outstretched, causing waste.

[9] For a quick read on the Progressive Era, see http://en.wikipedia.org/wiki/Progressive_Era

[10] F.W. Taylor, *The Principles of Scientific Management*, W.W. Norton & Company, New York, NY, 1911. For a biography of Mr. Taylor, see http://en.wikipedia.org/wiki/Frederick_Winslow_Taylor

[11] S. Kato, "Mr. Shigeo Shingo's P-Course and Contribution to TPS," http://www.superfactory.com/articles/kato_shingo.htm, July 2006

[12] J. Huntzinger, "The Roots of Lean," http://www.superfactory.com/articles/Huntzinger_roots_lean.pdf, June 2005, and A. Smalley, "TWI Influence on TPS and Kaizen," http://www.superfactory.com/articles/Smalley_Kato_TWI.htm, *May 2006*

[13] T. Peterson, "Hiroshi Okuda: 'Toyota Always Has a Sense of Crisis'," *BusinessWeek*, 25 April 2000, http://www.businessweek.com/bwdaily/dnflash/apr2000/nf00425e.htm and "Toyota Nearly No. 1, So Why Is Its Chief So Nervous?" *The Nikkei Weekly*, 21 August 2006

[14] *Lean Lexicon*, Third Edition, version 3.0, Lean Enterprise Institute, Cambridge, MA, p. 100

[15] J. Womack and D. Jones, "Lean Consumption," *Harvard Business Review*, March 2005, Vol. 83, No. 3, pp. 58-68, April 2001

[16] Where Lean is understood as a management system comprised of two principles: "Continuous Improvement" and "Respect for People," as defined in "The Toyota Way 2001," Toyota Motor Corporation, internal document, Toyota City, Japan, April 2001.

[17] S. Ghoshal, "Bad Management Theories are Destroying Good Management Practices," *Academy of Management Learning and Education*, Vol. 4, No. 1, 2005, pp. 75-91

[18] F. Ferraro, J. Pfeffer, and R. Sutton, "Economics Language and Assumptions: How Theories Can Become Self-Fulfilling," *Academy of Management Review*, Vol. 30, No. 1, 2005, pp. 8-24

Six questions about "The Tragedy of Waste" from Luke Van Dongen, which appeared on the Lean Blog (http://kanban.blogspot.com) on 7 November 2006.

Question 1 – What prompted you to begin your study of industrial management and engineering texts between 1910 and 1930? Was it pure curiosity or did something lead you to want to look back?

Answer – I have been interested in the history of Toyota and their management system for some time, and several years ago I began collecting the dozen or so out-of-print books written by former Toyota executives. I decided to go further backwards in time to better understand how the people who followed Frederick Winslow Taylor comprehended, systematized, and expanded upon his ideas.

Taylor's "Scientific Management" soon turned into "efficiency engineering," which then evolved into "industrial engineering." This lineage directly connects to Toyota's production system, as well as to its overall management system. It is very useful to learn what people at that time understood about waste, unevenness, and unreasonableness, its impact on the company and country, and the principles, processes, and tools they used to eliminate these losses.

Question 2 – In many of the quotes you selected to include in your article from the book, Chase refers to disciplines such as psychology, economics and sociology, in addition to engineering, as important in the pursuit of waste elimination. How do you view these relative to the pursuit of Lean management today?

Answer – Chase knew what he was talking about, and was correct to identify functioning, as well as broken, interconnections between these four knowledge areas, depending upon whether waste elimination was being pursued or not. Based upon my 12+ years of study of Toyota's management system, these knowledge areas are indeed interconnected and they strongly influenced the evolution of TPS. Clear evidence of this can be found in "The Toyota Way 2001" document, which describes Toyota's "fundamental DNA."

Knowledge of the interconnections is very important because it affects how we comprehend and practice Lean management. Ignorance of the interconnections is common today and leads to poor comprehension of Lean management, which typically results in the practice of "Fake Lean."

Question 3 – I found it striking that Chase readily recognized the existence of waste outside of the factory. Aside from Chase's examples, such as milk delivery in Rochester, New York, are there any lessons from the past that might be valuable to people working today to implement Lean in service and other settings?

Answer – Taylor and his successors were all well aware of the applicability of Scientific Management to any type of organization or activity. Then, like now, the principal focus was the factory because the improvements made there had a big positive impact that everyone could see. Then, as now, it was thought that making a big positive impact would deliver legions of converts, from associates to the CEO. Well, we know from our own experience what other people learned a long time ago: making a big impact does not yield many converts. I'll soon write an article that highlights the actions taken by a 1900's-era efficiency engineering consultant to gain top management buy-in. It will be very enlightening (see Chapter 11).

In general, the lessons from the past are the same as the lessons of today, whether in manufacturing or service businesses: take a scientific approach to understanding problems and applying countermeasures. That is: observe, gather data, make fact-based decisions, simplify processes, do root cause analysis, establish standard work, use visual controls, balance loads, be persistent, lead the organization in the least-waste way (in terms of leadership behaviors), etc.

Question 4 – Do you think Chase's concept of a "functional society" as it applies to a standard for measuring waste holds validity today?

Answer – To some extent it does, because a "functional society" is concerned about making ends meet as a society, with a little left over, which most people recognize as beneficial in an individual or family setting. Chase said that waste should not be measured in dollars, but in units of measure such as pounds, feet, time, etc. It is good advice that many people ignore to this day, and instead seek to attach a dollar figures to every kaizen.

Measuring in dollars means people at all levels of an organization will not learn to see and figure out how to eliminate the less obvious forms of waste (and unevenness and unreasonableness). Importantly, they will not learn a fundamental skill of Lean management, which is the constant interplay between "Continuous Improvement" and "Respect for People." Orry Fiume, retired CFO of the Wiremold Company, recognized this. He has long said: "Don't bean count Lean." It is free advice, worth millions and millions and millions of dollars.

Question 5 – You bring forth many concepts from Chase in your article, and relate these to modern terms for similar perhaps more evolved concepts used today such as Lean consumption. Did you come across anything in your research from the past that has not yet been translated into the present?

Answer – I think the fact that Chase and others had conceived the outline of what we today call "Lean consumption" is very interesting. It is one of many, many examples which illustrates that great ideas are often not as new as we think they are. One thing Chase talked about that is re-emerging is the linkage between economics and psychology, which today is called "behavioral economics." For the last 50 years or so, this linkage has been weak or non-existent in economics research and education, and likely explains, at least in part, why Lean remains out of the mainstream of management education and practice today.

Question 6 – You clearly identify political thinking and trends as interdependent factors that have in the past, and possibly continue today, to hinder the widespread adoption of Lean management. In your view, is a "Lean mindset" analogous to a "left-of-center" political characterization today? If so, is this a condition that must be overcome for Lean management to truly take hold?

Answer – It is possible that the "left-of-center" characterization could still be with us today, 81 years after Chase's book was published, though perhaps more on a subconscious level. However, I personally do not view the Lean mindset as "left-of-center." Lean embraces so much common sense thinking, rooted in observation and confronting facts and reality, that it transcends, or should transcend, political characterization. I touched upon this point in a recent article on Lean government (see Chapter 14).

If the "left-of-center" characterization does prevent Lean management from taking hold today, it would be only one of many causes that lead to the effect we see. For example, the industrial engineering books from 1910-1930, as well leadership books from the same period, reveal that corporate executives often ignored modern management ideas and methods. The authors identified many different causes, though not in a systematic manner. The problem of how to get senior management's attention, and their commitment and steady participation, long-term, is not new.

It could turn out that the political characterization is a very important factor. Perhaps economic theory over the last 50 years plays a larger role, or maybe the effect is driven by our current conception of the purpose of the corporation (e.g. shareholder supremacy vs. stakeholder balance). All of these causes are interrelated and also linked to psychology, social constructs, and business decision-making. Importantly, the strength of their influence upon senior managers depends upon the times in which they live. It is not difficult to identify causal factors linked to contemporary corporate, economic, or political theories which could be seen as inconsistent, in small or large ways, with the Lean management principles "Continuous Improvement" and "Respect for People."

10 Too Much Selfish Thinking

*The Lean community has struggled for many years to gain
buy-in from senior executives in large corporations.
Perhaps it's been so hard because there is too much
selfish thinking and not enough Lean thinking.
If so, what countermeasures can be applied?*

There is no doubt that Lean management has been mischaracterized as a "manufacturing thing" for most of the last 30 years, with a nearly singular focus on continuous improvement and the use Lean tools [1]. This has been a principal factor that has limited the application of Lean principles and practices beyond operations, and also, of course, into services businesses, government, non-profits, etc. It also helps explain why nearly 30 years after Lean came to America there are only a few big businesses that practice Lean management pretty well. Shouldn't there be many more?

Taiichi Ohno told us that Lean (TPS) was a *management system* in 1988 [2]. Yet it is only within the last few years that the larger community of Lean practitioners has started to realize this. However, a very small community of president and CEO-level Lean practitioners at The Jacobs Manufacturing Company and The Wiremold Company in Connecticut knew this in the late 1980's and early 1990's [3]. For nearly 20 years they, and some others, have been passionate advocates of Lean as a management system, yet few presidents or CEOs of big companies have listened [4].

The question is how do you get presidents and CEOs on

board? The general nature of the problem is one of trying to get people to think and work differently – to better serve the interests of customers first, as well as employees, investors, suppliers, and even management itself. It's definitely not a new problem.

The late 1800's and early 1900's were a time in which industrial management practices underwent a transformation to "modern methods" of management based upon the work of Frederick Winslow Taylor [5] and others. Scientific Management, as it was called, involved the application of the scientific method to understand business problems and improve workplace efficiency. Previously, most managers lacked quantitative data and information and thus often relied on hunches and educated guessed to manage their business. By the early 1900's, Scientific Management evolved into "efficiency engineering" with its main focus being optimization of a single process (i.e. point optimization), and then later "industrial engineering" whose focus expanded to system optimization – i.e. improvement of interrelated processes.

Dexter Kimball, in his 1913 book *Principles of Industrial Organization* [6] – an early text on industrial engineering and management – tackled the problem of how to get people to think and work differently. He, like Taylor and many others, knew that overcoming resistance was the key to achieving enterprise-wide improvements. While Kimball's focus was to convince laborers of the benefits of using modern methods to improve efficiency and effectiveness, the same problem existed for top management [5,7,8]. Most senior managers were dismissive of Scientific Management, much to the chagrin of its advocates who could see so clearly the wide-ranging benefits of process improvement.

The problem the industrial engineering community faced 100 years ago is largely the same as that faced by the Lean community today.

Kimball said in his book (insert the word "CEO" or "manager" for "worker"):

> "Why does the worker naturally resist these new methods? First, because the great majority of men are naturally afraid of all new things that they do not understand and the effects they cannot clearly foresee...

> Secondly, the worker may object to these new methods because of his inherent inertia. The workman who has once learned and long practiced certain methods of doing work is seldom willing to admit that a better way may be devised if these ways appear to be radically different from those to which he is accustomed.

> And lastly, he naturally opposes these new methods because his own experience and his inherited point of view naturally lead him to suspect any new methods that promise increased remuneration [or better outcomes] for increased efforts."

Kimball did not present a formal root cause analysis to support his conclusion that people are: 1) afraid of new things, 2) inherently resistant to new methods, and 3) suspicious that they might not be rewarded for their efforts. But if you do a fishbone diagram, these three items should appear.

Kimball's countermeasures were:

> "The first two objections may, perhaps, be removed by educational methods but the third is deep rooted... The basis of this objection is distrust, and the root of distrust is most usually selfishness... [overcoming this involves] the application of the **'fair deal'** on the part of all concerned."

In this explanation, he cites selfishness as a principal root cause of distrust, but items 1) and 2), above, are also related to selfishness. So let's focus exclusively on selfishness, recognizing that there are other factors, and see where it takes us.

Now is selfishness a root cause or a symptom? Let's start by asking: "Who teaches us about selfishness and when?" The obvious answer is our parents, who teach us about the antithesis of selfishness – sharing – in our earliest years through at least high school. We also learn about selfishness from our grade school teachers, the school books we read, and in religious instruction. The aim of all this training is to teach us that selfishness is bad and that sharing is the better value to embody. It's important to note that for most young people, teachings about sharing are probably intermittent; that is, sharing is typically reinforced only when we fail to share.

After we are educated in school we enter a second phase of life: our adult life. A major part of our adult life is our working life; the time and effort we apply at work to earn a living. The workplace is a very serious setting, as our livelihood and quality of life depends on our ability to fit in and make meaningful workplace contributions over 30 or 40 years. Now let's ask the same question: "Who teaches us about selfishness and when?"

Many of us are exposed to different values and standards of conduct at work than what we experienced growing up at home. This is partly reflected in the popular sayings that we often hear at work: "It's a dog-eat-dog world;" "I don't care how you do it, just get it done;" "Failure is not an option;" and "We play to win." Lots people say these things, including senior managers to whom we are likely to listen. These sayings reinforce the serious nature of the workplace, and are also indicative of a less sharing and thus more selfish environment.

There are other important influences such as business publications – *The Wall Street Journal*, *BusinessWeek*, and *Fortune* magazine – which many senior managers read. These often feature articles of senior managers who have successfully achieved some manner of point optimization. They often speak highly of the "tough guy, take no prisoners" type of leaders in the mold of "Chainsaw" Al Dunlap and Linda Wachner, or Carlos Ghosn and Jack Welch. If these publications approve of their approach to business, management, and leadership, why shouldn't we?

Another source that can greatly influence us is our college professors, perhaps especially so if we have earned an undergraduate or graduate degree from a business school. Among the most influential professors in the last 20-30 years have been those who teach economics and finance – lots of stuff related to point optimization. So we can see there are many influences that impinge upon us which shape our thinking and actions as managers.

Is it reasonable to say we are more likely to be selfish at work? Yes, it probably is. Just think of the internal battles that regularly take place between departments or company divisions over budgets, staffing, space, capital equipment, etc. Think too about the internal systems, processes, and metrics within each functional area that drive point optimization, day in and day out. And what about the external battles between corporations in which ethical and legal lines (e.g. anti-trust) are sometimes crossed. Aren't these all forms of selfish individual or corporate behavior? Importantly, these teachings are not intermittent. Instead, they are reinforced just about every day, and in a setting where we may have no other choice but to conform to the inefficiency and waste brought upon us by selfishness.

To many managers, selfishness may make more sense than sharing given the reality they experience every day at work. Beyond making sense, selfishness may be a practical response to harsh corporate environments. And it may even be necessary response, for if their supervisor or CEO is selfish and protective of his or her interests, then it would be wise from the perspective of survival to behave the exact same way. The workplace is obviously a very different type of environment than the home with respect to sharing.

In some ways we are all selfish, either as individuals or as managers, whether at work or at home. We all want to perpetuate ourselves and prosper. So perhaps it is better to think of selfishness as a spectrum with a low end and a high end. From the standpoint of values and integrity, it would be better to be at the low end or at least near the low end on the spectrum to avoid causing harm.

According to industrial psychologists, many managers exhibit sociopathic (also called psychopathic) behaviors [9]. It means to behave in ways that are anti-social: i.e. self-centered on one's own needs and lack of concern for how their behavior affects others. Selfishness may simply be a symptom that is rooted in the perceived benefits of point optimization of self, department, division, or company.

We all know the unfortunate but popular phrase: "Lean and Mean." It accurately portrays defective derivative forms of Lean – in essence, shortcuts (i.e. "cheats") – used by many managers over the years which result in zero-sum outcomes. That is to say, there must be winners and losers, as in: "Heads I win, tails you lose." Lean is indeed mean when the company and its managers reap the benefits of workers efforts to eliminate waste and then lay them off. Is that not sociopathic behavior at the high end of the spectrum?

In contrast, managers who have a correct understanding of Lean do not favor point optimization. They like to improve the entire system, one step at a time. And they seek non-zero sum outcomes that have many winners and no losers [10].

Lean management is fundamentally rooted in the practical, not idealistic, view that thoughtful sharing leads to greater prosperity and better outcomes. The objective is to promote desired reciprocal behaviors within the network of stakeholders – i.e. get people to work with you rather than against you – to enable learning in order to reduce system costs and continuously improve quality, flexibility, and innovation [11].

Examples of sharing in Lean management abound. Executives who understand Lean management well exhibit the following unselfish behaviors:

- Have profit-sharing programs
- Don't mind getting their hands dirty
- Like to experiment via kaizen
- Are humble and have little interest in the trappings of executive life
- They like to share information, ideas, and their knowledge
- Promote teamwork
- Support cross-training
- Look for similarities instead of amplifying differences
- Are externally focused, customer first, not themselves first
- View mistakes and problems as ways to improve, vs. blaming others which is selfish
- Seek to cooperate with labor, suppliers, etc., and mutually prosper
- Have reward systems based on teamwork
- Support standardization vs. "do your own thing"
- Lower barriers to communication between management and associates
- View associates as assets, not costs to be eliminated
- Act as teachers
- Have a broader sense of purpose vs. a narrow focus on making money
- Support consensus-building
- Believe in mutual trust
- Have respect for people

There's more. Don't forget the common trait among Lean people to freely share their success, failures, and new techniques, to collaborate, and to give credit where credit is due. Recall the three principles of kaizen: 1) process and results, 2) systemic thinking, and 3) non-blaming, non-judgmental [12]. These encourage sharing, while the results-focused approach common in business today encourages hoarding. Andon lights, used correctly, identify problems shared by the entire team, not just one worker or supervisor. Kaizen teams are cross-functional, which indicates problems belong to the company, not one individual or department. Lastly, what about sharing of knowledge and cost savings between a Lean company and its suppliers [13]? Need I go on?

The concept and practice of sharing is deeply embedded in Lean management. Putting the "Respect for People" principle into daily practice is an unselfish act that makes the other principle, "Continuous Improvement," possible. Unselfish human behaviors lead to unselfish corporate behaviors, which lead to a wide range of new opportunities and non-zero sum outcomes that most managers have great difficulty comprehending.

Lean management must be fundamentally unappealing, perhaps even repulsive, to senior managers who exhibit strong selfish characteristics and who have spent their career winning at point optimization. But that's not all that can be seen as unappealing.

Lean is learning and practice intensive. It takes years to understand the many nuances and interconnections between Lean principles, tools, practices, and the various internal and external stakeholders that interact with a business. That can be a turn-off to managers who have really big egos (again, selfish) who think they know it all (selfish, again). It requires undoing a lot of expensive and time-consuming learning that seemed to be very useful for many years. Why bother? Look where it got them. Most managers, it seems, are not willing to let go of what they know – yet another selfish behavior.

So let's return the problem which is, after nearly 30 years there are few big businesses that practice Lean well. A root cause for this problem is the belief among senior leaders that point optimization of self, department, division, or company is best. What countermeasures can be applied to correct this mistaken belief [14]?

Countermeasure #1. Recall Kimball's first countermeasure, education. This seems to be an appropriate countermeasure, though we might be dissatisfied with how long it takes to bear fruit given the way we currently conceptualize and practice educating people – courses, training sessions, books, videos, simulations, etc. However, isn't it somewhat predictable that these types of Lean education would be mostly ineffective at changing someone's beliefs? After all, this educational approach can appear theoretical to management practitioners. It is certainly worthwhile to continue efforts to educate people along these lines for future leadership positions [15], but it is clearly insufficient. Though, it would help to also teach managers the importance and periodic need to unlearn, as professionals in others fields understand the need to do when better information comes along – for example, in science and engineering [16] – to avoid repeating errors.

Countermeasure #2. Kimball's second countermeasure was

"...the application of the **'fair deal'** on the part of all concerned." This countermeasure circles back onto the problem at hand, namely that managers who perceive point optimization to be the preferred approach are not likely to be interested in fair deals. However, as the executive is the occupant of a higher position and perhaps better educated than the worker, they should at minimum be able to get the fundamentals right such as recognizing unfairness as a wasteful repeat error. They could also recognize the sensibility of responding to the pull of workers desires for fair deals. Perhaps an additional countermeasure would be for top managers adopt physicians' oath: "First, do no harm" [17].

Countermeasure #3. One thing we do know for certain is that people learn Lean principles and practices mostly by doing, and also that most executives do not participate in kaizen. Seeing is believing. But if top managers don't see, then how can they believe? So the route to changing the beliefs that lead to selfish behaviors gives us the third countermeasure: engage senior managers in a steady stream of individual and group kaizen [14,18]. This has historically been difficult to do, so the causes of non-participation need to be closely studied. But if they do participate, among the many things they will learn is their environment is less resource constrained then they think – which makes sharing much less of a problem.

Countermeasure #4. Of all the presidents and CEOs in the top 2000 U.S. corporations, there has to be at least one hundred who for many years have been unhappy with how business is generally conducted. They know in their heart there must be better ways to manage which are more consistent with their personal beliefs about sharing, cooperation, making system-wide improvements, improving human relations, etc., but don't know what to do or think it's just too hard to do. The fourth countermeasure would be to find those types of senior leaders and apply countermeasures 1, 2, and 3.

Lastly, an inescapable fact is that Lean management involves daily learning and never-ending practice [19]. Senior managers have to be hungry to learn and also eager to apply their new knowledge at work. Unfortunately there probably isn't much that can be done with the large population of presidents and CEOs who are not interested in Lean. They can't be forced to learn Lean management, unless perhaps customers or employees demand it. Even then, however, it will be an uphill struggle because current leadership practice, supported by business school teachings over the last 30 years [20], encourages many beliefs and behaviors that are the opposite those needed to correctly practice Lean management.

Notes

[1] See "Origins of Lean Management in America: The Role of Connecticut Businesses", by M.L. Emiliani, *Journal of Management History*, Vol. 12, No. 2, pp. 167-184 2006, http://www.theclbm.com/articles/lean_in_conn.pdf

[2] Ohno said: "Companies make a big mistake in implementing the Toyota production system thinking that it is just a production method. The Toyota production method won't work unless it is used as an overall management system... those who decide to implement the Toyota production system must be fully committed. If you try to adopt only the 'good parts', you'll fail." T. Ohno in *NPS: New Production System*, by I. Shinohara, Productivity Press, Cambridge, MA, 1988, p. 153 and 155.

[3] B. Emiliani, with D. Stec, L. Grasso, and J. Stodder, *Better Thinking, Better Results: Case Study and Analysis of an Enterprise-Wide Lean Transformation, Second Edition*, The CLBM, LLC, Wethersfield, Conn., 2007.

[4] O.J. Fiume and A. Byrne, personal communication.

[5] F.W. Taylor, *The Principles of Scientific Management*, W.W. Norton & Company, New York, NY, 1911. A much better expression of Taylor's thinking on Scientific Management is contained in his testimony to Congress in 25-30 January 1912. In his testimony, he repeatedly noted that the biggest challenge was management's resistance to obtaining a "new mental attitude," that being 90% of the problem. Taylor said there could be no Scientific Management if the new mental attitude did not exist among the top managers of a company. See *Scientific Management: Comprising Shop Management, Principles of Scientific Management, Testimony Before the House Committee*, F.W. Taylor, with Foreword by Harlow S. Person, Harper & Brothers Publishers, New York, NY, 1947

[6] D. Kimball, *Principles of Industrial Organization*, McGraw-Hill Book Company, New York, NY, 1913, pp. 264-265.

[7] C.E. Knoeppel, *Installing Efficiency Methods*, The Engineering Magazine Co., New York, NY, 1917.

[8] W. Basset, *Taking the Guesswork Out of Business*, The B.C Forbes Publishing Company, New York, NY, 1924. Basset's book begins with a Preface by Samuel Crowther, a noted business journalist who co-authored Henry Ford's books: *My Life and Work* (1922) and *Today and Tomorrow* (1926). Crowther says: "The biggest thing we have learned about industry in the last twenty-odd years is that the work must flow as continuously as a river flows from its source to the sea... Henry Ford found that it paid to do away with the little dams that used to be inside a business and to keep the work flowing through the factory." (p. v)

[9] P. Kaihla, "Getting Inside the Boss's Head," *Business 2.0*, pp. 49-51, Vol. 4, No. 10, November 2003, http://money.cnn.com/magazines/business2/business2_archive/2003/11/01/351936/index.htm. See also A. Deutschman, "Is Your Boss a Psychopath?," *Fast Company*, July 2005, p. 44, http://www.fastcompany.com/magazine/96/open_boss.html.

[10] In the imperfect real world there may indeed be some losers, but skilled Lean managers seek to reduce their numbers and also minimize their pain.

[11] Promoting opportunistic behaviors and conflict among network participants is wasteful, self-defeating, and just plain stupid. See References 1, 3, and 13 for guidance on how to avoid such problems.

[12] M. Imai, "Kaizen Seminar", Hartford Graduate Center, Hartford, Conn., May 1988.

[13] J. Dyer and K. Nobeoka, "Creating and Managing a High Performance Knowledge-Sharing Network: They Toyota Case," *Strategic Management Journal*, Vol. 21, pp. 345-367, 2000.

[14] For more on the differences in beliefs between conventional managers and Lean managers, see "Linking Leaders' Beliefs to Their Behaviors and Competencies," M.L. Emiliani, *Management Decision*, Vol. 41, No. 9, 2003, pp. 893-910.

[15] See http://www.teachinglean.org for information on the network of college educators bringing Lean into the classroom.

[16] It seems that scientists and engineers are more willing to unlearn important concepts or practices because they believe the new knowledge will help them do their jobs better. In contrast, many senior managers seem to dislike unlearning important concepts or practices because they are not sure if the new knowledge will help them do their job better.

[17] M.L. Emiliani, "The Oath of Management," *Management Decision*, Vol. 38, No. 4, 2000, pp. 261-262.

[18] M.L. Emiliani and D.J. Stec, "Using Value Stream Maps to Improve Leadership," *Leadership and Organizational Development Journal*, Vol. 25, No. 8, pp. 622-645, 2004.

[19] S. Spear, "Learning to Lead at Toyota," *Harvard Business Review*, Vol. 82, No. 5, 2004, pp. 78-86.

[20] See M.L. Emiliani, "Improving Management Education," *Quality Assurance in Education*, Vol. 14, No. 4, 2006, pp. 363-384 and M.L. Emiliani, "Is Management Education Beneficial to Society?," *Management Decision*, Vol. 42, No. 3/4, 2004, pp. 481-498.

11 Gaining Executive Buy-In for Lean

*Gaining executive buy-in for process improvement activities
has been a major challenge for over 100 years.
Taking a trip back in time to see how an experienced
improvement engineer handled this problem can provide
useful insights for today's challenges.*

In 1914, Charles E. Knoeppel wrote a series of articles in *The
Engineer Magazine* that focused on the actual practice of putting efficiency methods into place in a typical manufacturing
business. The series of articles was very popular, and three
years later they were expanded and published as a book titled
Installing Efficiency Methods [1]. The book set out to answer
two questions (p. i):

- "What is the first thing an efficiency engineer does
  when he comes into a plant on the first morning of his
  engagement – and what is the next thing, and the next,
  and the next?
- How does he find out where to begin the work of betterment, and what does he do when he has found it?"

Knoeppel explains how to do this step-by-step in each of the
29 chapters of the book. He was able to write this book
because he had years of experience as a shop laborer and
drafter, and later as a self-taught management consultant specializing in efficiency engineering. He was part of the community of practice-oriented process improvement engineers
led by Frederick Winslow Taylor, who wrote the book *The
Principles of Scientific Management* [2].

Knoeppel's interest was to help labor and management work together to improve the efficiency of both shop and office work. He felt that management practitioners needed additional resources to better understand and apply efficiency methods. Part of the motivation for writing such a book was no doubt related to the great difficulty people like Knoeppel had experienced in gaining top management buy-in. In 1912, Frederick Taylor said in testimony to Congress [3]:

> "...nine-tenths of our trouble has been to 'bring' those on the management's side to do their fair share of the work and only one-tenth of our trouble has come on the workman's side."

Thus, a countermeasure for overcoming management resistance was to write a detailed "how-to" book. Knoeppel begins the Preface of the book by reflecting upon when he first became a consultant (p. iii):

> "It seemed strange to me that almost invariably a manufacturer had to be coaxed into accepting better methods."

Strange indeed. He went on to say:

> "Instead of deciding a case on its merits, instead of doing a thing because it was good business to do it, the campaign was one of doing what was expedient, often unnecessary, and many times wrong. It was necessary to worship the god 'diplomacy,' and if a man possessed tact, ability became a secondary consideration. What was done was with the consent of the organization. Opposition, sometimes passive, sometimes active, was

often encountered. Heart failure would have resulted if a manager had said: 'Here is the factory; you have been found competent to introduce efficient methods; go ahead'."

One can understand Knoeppel's consternation regarding the placement of qualifications and ability as secondary. Managers often talk a good line about hiring based on merit, but experience suggests that other, less meaningful decision-making criteria are actually more prominent.

Knoeppel continues:

"The word 'efficiency' has been juggled until it has lost its real meaning simply because it stands for any-thing that a person wants it to mean. Because of the mystery with which the methods have been enveloped it is viewed with suspicion and distrust. Failures have been many. In some cases the engineers have been responsible, but case after case could be cited that would convict the client of 'contributory negligence'."

It seems that not much has changed in nearly 100 years. Today, there is much confusion over the meaning of Lean, and Lean is widely viewed with suspicion and distrust.

"The profession [efficiency engineering consulting] has not been altogether professional... Men with a copy of Emerson's *Twelve Principles of Efficiency* and Taylor's *Shop Management*, plus a prayer, have been able to convince unsuspecting clients that they knew exactly what these clients wanted and were prepared to give it to them."

Knoeppel bemoans the lack of professionalism, knowledge, and capability among efficiency consultants. He goes on to say:

> "Why this condition? My whole experience has taught me that one thing stands out above all else as the real reason: *Lack of a thorough understanding of the proposition both as regards to the work itself and the methods followed by the men identified with the* [scientific management] *movement.*"

So the challenge was to inform executives of the process for installing efficiency methods and the type of person who was competent to do this work.

> "It therefore seemed to me that what the industrial world needed most was a work of such a practical nature as not only to induce managers to investigate it and try it out in small ways in their own business, but to serve in an indirect way to furnish the measure of the men competent to handle the details. Knowing more about the the proposition themselves, they [managers] would be in a better position to gauge the ability and success of the [efficiency] engineer."

Thus, Knoeppel's primary audience for the book is company executives, whereas the articles he had written previously in *The Engineer Magazine* were intended for working-level engineers. The idea of writing a detailed "how-to" book for executives is as appealing today as it was in 1917. In the context of Lean management, there are many new authors, myself included [4] whose target audience is senior managers. While it remains worthwhile to write such books, experience reveals that it is not sufficient for overcoming resistance to Lean management among top managers, in part because most senior managers do not read books.

Knoeppel concludes the Preface by saying:

> "… it is hoped that in some measure this book will open the eyes of executives to the value of the work – so necessary to our industrial progress."

There is probably no doubt that Knoeppel's book favorably impacted some top managers and the companies they owned or worked for. And one can easily say that industrial progress has been made along many dimensions since 1917. However, it can also be said that progress along the dimension of fundamental process improvement – the elimination of waste, unevenness, and unreasonableness – has been isolated at best, and understood broadly by manufacturing managers only in times of national emergency such as World War I [5] and World War II [6].

More importantly, what knowledge of processes improvement people did possess has not carried over from one generation of managers to the next. Avoiding this outcome is one of the most amazing aspects of what Toyota has done. So overall, since the dawn of Scientific Management in 1882 [3], it is safe to say that managers have not paid much attention to process improvement. Instead, the focus has been on results, with little or no interest in process. The contraction of the American manufacturing base over the last 30 years, in large part due to executives searching for lower cost labor, is testament to this.

Unfortunately, what we have been engaged in is the constant re-introduction of process improvement principles and practices to each new generation of managers. Knoeppel and others from his day would marvel at the inefficiency. And they would probably be shocked to learn how their work has been misunderstood or ignored by educators.

Nevertheless, training each new generation of managers is work that has to be done – non-value added but necessary – if we hope to improve the performance of manufacturing (and service) businesses that remain in the U.S., as well as prepare for the days when some manufacturing may return to the U.S. The question is: Is there a better way? And then a better way after that? Let's look at what Knoeppel wrote in more detail.

In the first 5 chapters, Knoeppel presents a realistic and detailed narrative describing a company with declining profits that is headed for sale or bankruptcy. Top company officers fret about the problems that lie before them when the general manager suggests hiring a "consulting engineer on management and organization." The president of the company quickly rejects this idea, and says: "…a stranger who knows less than we do about it [our business] would only manage things in a way that would invite even greater disaster." A company director agrees with the president and cites three firms who had this type of work done and were very dissatisfied with the results. The general manager, however, skillfully points out flaws in each of the president's and director's arguments and convinces them to meet with a consultant.

The consultant, Mr. Brown, performs a diagnosis of the company through a series of questions to top company managers. Mr. Brown, in turn, gives detailed answers to the president's questions. The president is initially impressed, but asks Mr. Brown to provide additional examples from companies he has previously worked with. These detailed examples impress the president even more, as does the fact that Mr. Brown honestly responds to questions about the failures that he experienced in past assignments. Mr. Brown gets the job.

The remaining 21 chapters describe various plans of investigation and activity that a competent efficiency engineering consultant would carry out. The methodology is similar to how physicians diagnose and treat patients, with Mr. Brown acting as a "business doctor." Careful consideration is given to leadership and behavioral aspects of work and organization – what we today refer to as "organizational behavior" or "culture."

Before I elaborate on Knoeppel's method for gaining management buy-in, it is worthwhile noting the many aspects of efficiency engineering that are consistent with Lean management. The descriptions of the various plans of investigation and activity clearly show basic awareness or detailed knowledge of the following (though not necessarily in the same language as that used below):

- Waste – defects, transporting, waiting, and movement
- Unevenness
- Unreasonableness
- Variation
- Standardization
- Workflows and layout

- Teamwork
- Observation and "go see"
- Milk runs
- Ask why
- Load balancing
- Preventative maintenance
- Audio and visual controls
- Point-of-use
- Importance of good management-labor relations

Interestingly, there was also an awareness of "push" and "pull" in a discussion of how to plan work (p. 121):

> "The [planning] method outlined also leads to an important principle which all should work to and which will do much to correct the usual policy found in shops. It can be stated as follows: *The method to follow in getting the work though a shop is not to apply pressure at A towards B, but to draw at B from A.* This means a 'pull' type instead of a 'push' type, as one man expressed it."

Knoeppel also outlines how poor wage plans, poor working conditions, and poor human relations cause great inefficiencies. Thus, there was a clear recognition that certain policies and types of management thinking and behavior created waste. Regarding worker complaints, Knoeppel said (p. 232):

> "All bosh, you say, this listening to complaints. Let me cite cases that will show that it is a wise plan to listen to complaints, which after all *are suggestions of a reversed nature.*"

Finally, Knoeppel criticized the nearly uniform desire among executives to search for heroic individuals who can produce business results, rather than learn about the principles and related management practices that have been concretely demonstrated to improve efficiency (pp. 234-235):

> "It is hard to convince executives that law and principle can be made to operate successfully. As a manufacturer recently wrote me: 'What we think we really need more than anything else is a foreman who can produce results, and now we are trying out a man who thinks he can do this.' In other words, the manufacturer does not know what he needs to secure results... The phrase is the most eloquent summing up of the conditions existing in many of our manufacturing concerns that I have seen."

Now let's return to the methods used by Knoeppel to gain executive buy-in for process improvement. At the macro-level the obvious method was to write a practical how-to book for executives. The idea was to inform executives what to expect if they were thinking of hiring an efficiency consultant in order to reduce or remove their fears of the unknown. Along the way, Knoeppel described in detail what a competent and reputable efficiency consultant looked like and what he did.

At the micro-level, the book reveals a more formal strategy. First, Knoeppel presents a common business problem, declining profits, to impel action on the part of management. This is the well-known "crisis" scenario that Lean practitioners have long understood. While this is not new to us today, it may have been new in 1914 when the magazine articles were published. Next, Knoeppel presents Mr. Brown, the consultant, in a very measured and carefully designed way: first to gain management's trust through sound logic and reasoning, and then gain their buy-in for efficiency improvement activities. To do this, Mr. Brown had to possess the following characteristics:

- Ability to communicate to company officers in very direct and clear terms, orally, without lengthy reports as back-up documentation.
- Thoroughly answer questions from any direction, about any aspect of the business
- Deep, deep, deep knowledge of process improvement, with many practical examples, and the ability to explain how it intersects with human behaviors and needs, day-to-day work activities in various departments, management objectives, and business goals.

In order for executives to recognize these as desirable characteristics they had to be shown the details of what to look for. Knoeppel's book gave executives key insights and tips to generate buy-in and also knowledge they would need to interview candidate efficiency engineers and make smart purchasing decisions for consulting services.

There are other methods for gaining top management buy-in for Lean management that will, no doubt, continue, such as educating or informing people through books, articles, conference, meetings, degree and certificate programs [7], etc., and also through direct participation in process improvement activities. After all, seeing is believing.

What else could be done? One approach could be to establish

a coordinated effort to create pull for Lean among key stakeholders such as employees, suppliers, customers, and
investors for a particular company or industry segment. Lean
could more aggressively align itself with the public's growing
interest in green products and services and sustainable business practices. Lean management could assert itself more
strongly in the growing efforts to improve service productivity, and also exploit the intersections of Lean and information
technologies as Toyota Motor Corporation has done.

Another opportunity could be for large institutional investors,
who are influential among top executives, to establish and
fund a research organization similar in concept and purpose
to the Insurance Institute for Highway Safety or
Underwriter's Laboratories Inc. [8]. A necessary supporting
action would be to standardize leadership so that generations
of top executives understand how to create wealth from
waste, unevenness, and unreasonableness. These actions
might provide the push needed to gain broad-based buy-in for
REAL LEAN [9] among current and future Fortune 2000
executives.

Knoeppel conclusion to the book contains these sharp words
(pp. 236-237):

> "It is hoped that what has been said in this and previous
> chapters will convince executives that there is, after all,
> something of real and substantial value in this efficien-
> cy work. A writer recently said: 'As our industries are
> organized to-day, not one establishment in ten can have
> scientific management, because not one in ten is will-
> ing to live by its law.' If this is true, then the executives

of our industries are to blame. Whether or not the work is to be the success possible; whether or not our industrialism is to be the most efficient on earth – is simply a question of the co-operation of executives and managers. The engineer has been and is doing his share. His work is exceedingly trying, calls for considerable travel, and demands much in the way of personal sacrifice. He is constantly forced to battle with trying situations back of which are skepticism and doubt. Certainly opposition will not make his task any easier. That he will win there is no question, for the history of every movement shows that the things which are now successful were forced to withstand bitter criticism and repeated failures, some having to fight for their very existence... Because we are quitters; because we are skeptical of anything new; because in America there is too much 'each for himself' – the progress of the work to date is not all it should be. Industry and the community at large are the real losers – not the engineers and those who advocate what has been described in these pages... *it behooves industrial managers to cease condemning on general principles and to make a real and consistent attempt to find the meat that will prove to be the best kind of industrial nourishment"* [10].

Notes:

[1] C.E. Knoeppel, *Installing Efficiency Methods*, The Engineering Magazine Co., New York, NY, 1917. The Engineering Magazine was edited by Charles Buxton Going, who played an important role in establishing the profession of industrial engineering. See http://en.wikipedia.org/wiki/Charles_Buxton_Going.

[2] F.W. Taylor, *The Principles of Scientific Management*, W.W. Norton & Company, New York, NY, 1911.

[3] Taylor's philosophy of management and the principles and practices of Scientific Management are widely misunderstood. The best expression of his thinking can be found in his testimony to Congress given on 25-30 January 1912. See *Scientific Management: Comprising Shop Management, Principles of Scientific Management, Testimony Before the House Committee*, F.W. Taylor, with Foreword by Harlow S. Person, Harper & Brothers Publishers, New York, NY, 1947.

[4] B. Emiliani, with D. Stec, L. Grasso, and J. Stodder, *Better Thinking, Better Results: Case Study and Analysis of an Enterprise-Wide Lean Transformation, Second Edition*, The CLBM, LLC, Wethersfield, Conn., 2007.

[5] S. Chase, *The Tragedy of Waste*, The Macmillan Company, New York, NY, 1925.

[6] W. Vogt, "What You Can Do When You Have To" and "The Production Runs of the Century: A Comparison of Plant II and Willow Run," pp. 6-21, *Target*, Vol. 15, No. 1, First Quarter 1989.

[7] For more on what educators are doing to bring Lean management to the classroom, see http://www.teachinglean.org.

[8] This is one way in which insurers guard against losses. Couldn't institutional investors do the same? It might be a very effective supplement to risk management activities and state and government oversight (e.g. SEC, FTC, Justice Department).

[9] Where REAL LEAN embodies the principles "Continuous "Improvement" and "Respect for People," and Fake Lean is "Continuous Improvement" only. See "The Toyota Way 2001," Toyota Motor Corporation, internal document, Toyota City, Japan, April 2001.

[10] Around 1915, Knoeppel realized that his focus on process efficiency had limited appeal to company managers. So he shifted tactics and sought to gain senior managers' buy-in for efficiency improvement by showing them how to achieve greater profits. In 1937, Knoeppel and Edgar Seybold wrote a book titled *Managing for Profit: Working Methods for Profit Planning and Control* (McGraw-Hill, New York). The book introduced new graphical rep-

resentations of financial statements called "profitgraphs" for the income statement and "capitalgraphs" for the balance sheet. He also introduced his new profit formula: income – profit = allowable expense (vs. the usual profit formula: income – expense = profit [or loss]). Knoeppel's new formula is what Lean people use in Target Costing activities (i.e. price – profit = cost). He also advocated the use of flexible or moving budgets instead of fixed or static budgets, which unfortunately are still widely used today. Knoeppel viewed static budgets as inherently defective because business is never static. The shortcoming of this book is that it presents a traditional view of absorption accounting and cost-volume relationships. Mr. Knoeppel died one month before the book was published.

12 Jefferson Pilot's Lean Initiative

Jefferson Pilot Financial's Lean implementation is heralded as great example of what to do. But upon closer examination, it is nothing more than the common approach to Lean implementation taken by most organizations. It contains many errors and perpetuates misunderstandings about Lean management.

A critique of
"The Lean Service Machine"
Harvard Business Review
Vol. 81, No. 10, pp. 123-129, 2003

At first reading, the manner in which Jefferson Pilot Financial introduced Lean principles and practices appears to be quite reasonable. But for those who know a lot about Lean transformations and the history of Lean, they see something different: a well-worn functional approach to implementation that does not deliver enterprise-wide benefits that end-use customers value.

Depending upon one's point of view, the common approach to Lean implementation can be full of "errors" or contain many "opportunities for improvement."

The stronger word "errors" is more suitable for conveying the likelihood that after reading the *Harvard Business Review* article, managers will gain an incorrect understanding of Lean. For that reason, the word "error" is used in this critique.

Comparing the article to The Wiremold Company's enterprise-wide Lean transformation [1] reveals common implementation errors. These can serve as improvement opportunities for other managers who are engaged in a Lean transformation:

- The CEO did not personally participate in kaizen. This typically conveys to people that participation by the CEO, and the rest of the senior management team, is not needed. It also indicates that the CEO is not really interested in Lean, and does not understand Lean as a management system for the entire organization.

- Initial implementation occurred in only one part of the organization – operations – and on a very small scale. This typically conveys to people outside of operations that Lean is an "operations thing," and that they do not need to participate or bother learning about Lean. It also indicates to people that being Lean in operations alone is good enough to gain competitive advantage.

- Implementation in only one part of the organization is a "local incremental" or point optimization approach often used to avoid disrupting the organization. While that may seem reasonable, it conveys to people that Lean should not be disruptive, when in fact it should be disruptive. Being disruptive helps people understand the massive amount of waste that exists in business processes. It gets people's attention.

- The "Lean team" was small – just five people, three of which were consultants – and not cross-functional. This conveys to people that Lean is the job of consultants, or only the people doing the work in that area are qualified to identify ways to improve the work. Kaizen teams are usually larger and contain people from upstream and downstream processes. People from outside the department invariably offer valuable insights and also learn many important new things.

- Posting metrics, performance vs. goal, on white boards is standard practice in Lean management to provide real-time visibility into the performance of the system. It should not be used for blaming people, as seems to be the case in the article. In a Lean transformation done right, the CEO establishes and adheres to a no-blame policy so that people at all levels will feel comfortable participating in kaizen and learning new Lean principles, processes, and tools.

- Who is the customer? There is usually much confusion on this point. The common view among life insurance company executives is that the customer is the independent life insurance advisors – also called "producers" or "sales reps". However, advisors themselves are not the source of future cash flows. The policyholder is. Advisors are a cost, with the first year or two of premiums being paid to the advisor. From a practical standpoint, the value proposition is defined by both advisors (distributors) and policyholders (end-use customers). The challenge is to expand the value proposition for both, not for one or the other. Most policyholders, if asked, would probably like to obtain better life insurance coverage for less money. Lean done right in the life insurance business will lower costs, which will translate into better value for policyholders.

- The choice of words used in articles tells a lot about how writers think about Lean, which will then influence how readers think about and practice Lean. Using the words "initiative" or "project" indicate to people that Lean has a definable end point – that soon you'll be done. It's no accident that Lean is often referred to as "a journey" because there is no end to improvement. Also, calling Lean an "initiative" does not convey to people that Lean is a management system for the entire business. The words "optimal design" indicates to people there is one best solution, and thus conflicts with the "Continuous Improvement" principle. The word "tools" indicate to people Lean is just that – a bunch of tools – versus a management system rooted in principles ("Continuous Improvement" and "Respect for People"), with objectives such as create value for end-use customers, stable long-term growth, balance/harmony, and innovation, and supported by processes and tools such as kaizen, QFD, standard work, root cause analysis, TPM, etc.

- Why implement Lean to begin with? For most senior managers, the main reason is to increase earnings through cost reduction, and thus increase stock price. This conveys to people Lean is just another tool in manager's tool kit to cut costs. Improved financials are a byproduct of improving the non-financial performance of value streams. Non-financial measures are the focus of cell-level Lean metrics. Importantly, having a purely financial view of the benefits of Lean undercuts the "Respect for People" principle and does not help people focus on improving business processes.

- While the Airplane Game and similar types of Lean simulations are popular, Lean businesses do not use them because they do not: a) develop people's capability to observe and discern between value-added work, non-value added but necessary work, and waste in actual business processes; b) eliminate waste in actual business processes; c) create value for end-use customers; and d) change people's belief system. In short, it does not create conditions necessary for learning and behavioral changes in the actual work environment. Kaizen applied to actual business processes is the day-to-day teaching method, not games.

- Labor costs were reduced by 26%. What happened to the people? Did senior management offer all associates a "Qualified Job Guarantee" - i.e. nobody will be laid off as a direct result of their participation in continuous improvement activities? If no "Qualified Job Guarantee" was given, then this undercuts the "Respect for People" principle.

While these errors are common, they are not caused by bad intentions. Rather, they are due to a lack of awareness of improved practical Lean implementation methods, the difficulty that most senior managers have discerning between Lean and non-Lean principles and practices, and underestimating the ease with which confusing mixed messages can be delivered.

Notes

[1] B. Emiliani, with D. Stec, L. Grasso, and J. Stodder, *Better Thinking, Better Results: Case Study and Analysis of an Enterprise-Wide Lean Transformation, Second Edition*, The CLBM, LLC, Wethersfield, Conn., 2007.

13 Lean in Higher Education

The time is right for higher education administrators,
faculty, and staff to begin applying Lean management
to their business. The consequences of not
doing so could be fatal.

Most U.S. colleges and universities face a never-ending struggle to deliver valuable educational services while at the same
time maintaining a viable financial position. The normal route
for doing both is simply to raise more money from donors and
pass cost increases along to customers – not only students – or
their parents or the companies that students work for – but also
to the companies, state, and federal agencies that fund research.

This inexorable rise in prices, often at rates that greatly exceed
the rate of inflation, places unwanted burdens on those who
must pay the costs of education and research. This can't go on
forever. Surely factors will emerge in the near future that force
a change in current pricing practices and value propositions.

University administrators, faculty, and staff have a choice.
They can change voluntarily, in an orderly manner while the
opportunity exists to do so, or be forced to change when
power inevitably shifts to those who pay the bills. Every insti-
tution will be affected in some way – even the top-ranked
ones – and the shift could occur very rapidly as the cost to
deliver information and knowledge drops.

As the population of college-aged students begins to decline
in some regions of the U.S. after 2010, administrators will

face new challenges that they are not yet prepared to address. A likely scenario is:

- Oversupply of capable higher education service providers
- Degree programs that are not differentiated between competitors
- Growth of for-profit educational service providers
- Growth of the distance education market via the Internet
- Having to compete on the basis of price

In addition, education standards have become increasingly uniform across the globe, aided by international accreditation bodies such as AACSB International for business schools or ABET for engineering schools [1]. This means that undergraduate engineering or graduate business degree programs in U.S. schools are substantially the same as those offered by schools in Canada or Germany, or by schools in developing nations such as China or Poland (and also taught in English).

If most undergraduate and graduate degree programs are substantially the same, either in reality or perception, then wouldn't most senior corporate executives seek labor that provides the needed capability at the lowest price? Indeed, we are now witnessing the early stages of offshore outsourcing of white-collar "knowledge worker" jobs in information technology, human resources, finance, engineering, law, and medicine. The pace of offshoring white-collar jobs is certain to increase in the coming years and further build the global labor market. In addition to significant job losses, this will also depress the salaries of U.S.-based knowledge workers who are fortunate to retain their jobs.

If it does not pay to obtain an undergraduate or graduate degree, then some potential students will migrate to jobs that can not be outsourced offshore such as emergency medical technician, nurse, plumber, carpenter, electrician, hotel and restaurant services, etc. – honorable trades, to be sure. However, enrollment in degree programs will decline more quickly as potential students seek alternatives, and make a bad situation even worse. As a result, some schools will go out of business, some will merge with other schools, and others will exist for a period of time as zombie (half-dead, half-alive) schools.

University administrators, even those at top-tier U.S. schools, should be alarmed because what could happen to higher education is no different than what has already happened to the U.S. steel, electronics, automotive, furniture, and textile industries. And the same thing is now happening to service industries such as customer support, financial analysis, and drug research. While it is true that market dynamics often provide a useful and necessary culling of the weak players, it also offers compelling opportunities to improve and become even stronger.

It seems conditions are forming which could drastically alter the business of higher education as we know it today. Managing through this new phase will be an unpleasant task. So how can institutions willing to face this new reality adapt? One way they can is to do what managers usually do: they lay people off, eliminate programs, cut back on services, close branch campuses, etc. These worn-out solutions will lead to unhappy customers and higher levels of job dissatisfaction among those left to carry out the teaching and provide student services – and could also hasten the school's demise.

Is there a better way to deal with this situation? Of course there is. We need only to reflect on what some managers do when confronted with major upheaval in their industry. They begin to implement Lean management to reduce costs, improve quality, simplify processes, gain market share, stabilize or grow employment, and better satisfy customers.

The question is, will college and university administrators, faculty, and staff wait until the crisis lands upon them, or will they act now to improve?

Professors have written dozens of scholarly papers in recent years illustrating the application of Lean principles and practices to higher education, including: quality function deployment, hoshin kanri, and kaizen. They know there is waste in higher education.

So there are many people out there who want to improve, and are willing to lead the way. And it's not just faculty. Some administrators and most staff personnel also know there is much room for improving degree programs and related student services. But great ideas are not so great until they are transformed into broad-based action.

Inevitably, however, people in service businesses must overcome the common bias that Lean is a "manufacturing thing," and understand there are many more similarities than differences between manufacturing and service businesses. Administrators, faculty, and staff must avoid the trap of viewing higher education as a special case where Lean does not apply.

People who are not encumbered by mistaken views, and also accept that students are customers – in balance with the mission of higher education – will want to participate in kaizen to improve individual courses, degree programs, and student services. This will lead to multiple characteristics that clearly differentiate one school from others as seen by customers and lead to positive outcomes.

I think it is relevant to mention my own experience with Lean management in manufacturing and service industries. With the help of extensive training by Shingijutsu consultants in the mid-1990's, we learned and applied Lean management principles and practices in the manufacturing shop and later in supply chains.

Our teams achieved remarkable results, even though our understanding of Lean at that time was somewhat limited by our manufacturing shop floor focus. But we learned many important things about process improvement that laid the foundation for understanding how to improve non-manufacturing processes.

Upon becoming a university professor in the fall of 1999, it was clear to me there was an enormous amount of waste in all facets of higher education – admissions process, advising, individual courses, degree programs, student services, etc. So I did four things:

- Led efforts to reduce confusion and rework by simplifying the school's programs and requirements.

- Conducted seminars for faculty on Lean management

and important tools such as root cause analysis.

- Applied Lean principles and practices to the courses I taught [2] (with great success!).

- Gained the participation of faculty, staff, alumni, and senior managers to improve a graduate M.S. in management degree program using kaizen [3].

The rationale for improvement and related implementation efforts are described in recent papers that I have written (see notes 2 and 3). To make a long story short, Lean principles and practices can be successfully applied to higher education – which should be no surprise. We used improvement processes that were either exactly the same or very close to those long used in industrial manufacturing settings.

Another opportunity is to include Lean principles and practices in all courses – not just in operations management courses. This will result in curricula that teach students how to continuously improve any process and utilize human resources in ways that demonstrate respect for people [4]. It will produce graduates with clearly identifiable value-adding knowledge and capabilities such as creating innovative products or services and improving productivity through fundamental process improvement [5].

Further, students educated in Lean principles and practices – understanding waste, unevenness, and unreasonableness, value stream mapping, kaizen, respect for people, balance, etc. – will be much more highly valued by corporate managers because applying this knowledge leads to better outcomes for all key stakeholders. Plus, it will be harder to out-source their capabilities. And it will also clearly differentiate the programs offered by some U.S. colleges and universities.

But is important to be totally consistent: educators can't just teach Lean principles and practices, they must also apply it to their business.

By the way, another thing that U.S. college and university personnel will have to worry about is non-U.S. institutions of higher education adopting Lean principles and practices first, thus making both their schools and graduates more desirable than U.S. schools and its graduates.

So the message is: Don't miss this golden opportunity to apply Lean to university management, and also to teach Lean principles and practices to students across a variety of disciplines including arts, sciences, engineering, management, medicine, etc.

You can help by lobbying your alma mater to adopt Lean management.

Notes

[1] Predictably, neither AACSB International (www.aacsb.edu) nor ABET (www.abet.org) suggest or explicitly require educators to teach Lean principles and practices in their respective accreditation standards. This illustrates how obscure Lean is in higher education. Thus, educators have broad leeway to teach concepts, principles, tools, etc., that can maximize waste as well as those that eliminate waste. Unfortunately, teaching people the "least-waste way" to think, behave, and work are not yet highly regarded by accreditation bodies. Also, customer demand for this type of education is weak at the present time, in part because the value proposition has not been articulated.

[2] M.L. Emiliani, "Improving Business School Courses by Applying Lean Principles and Practices," *Quality Assurance in Education* , Vol. 12, No. 4, pp. 175-187, 2004.

[3] M.L. Emiliani, "Using Kaizen to Improve Graduate Business School Degree Programs," *Quality Assurance in Education*, Vol. 13, No. 1, pp. 37-52, 2005.

[4] Toyota Motor Corporation, "The Toyota Way 2001," internal document, Toyota City, Japan, April 2001.

[5] M.L. Emiliani, "Is Management Education Beneficial to Society?," *Management Decision*, Vol. 42, No. 3/4, pp. 481-498, 2004.

14 Lean Government – Crazy Dream or Absolute Necessity?

Wanted: Brave politicians, appointed officials, and career civil servants to join together to pioneer the application of Lean management to municipal, state, and federal government services.

Your property and payroll taxes keep going up, but your salary does not. Important government services are underfunded or cut, but your needs remain the same or may even expand. It does not seem to you that government services, overall, are getting any better. But don't worry, the U.S. Bureau of Labor statistics predicts that between 2002 and 2012, federal, state, and municipal government employment will grow by over 2.5 million jobs – with most of the increase coming from state and municipal governments [1]. Do you have confidence that hiring more people will help improve government services? Probably not.

Conventional wisdom says the problem is "big government," and the answer is "small government." Among the cognoscenti, the best pathway to smaller government is obvious: privatization, better known as outsourcing. Just turn over government services to private enterprises who, through the twin miracles of less government regulation and free market competition, will deliver the needed service at much lower cost. But is privatization always the best answer? A Lean thinker would closely examine the "big government" problem by asking "why?" several times to discover the root cause and identify countermeasures.

In some cases, privatization, through a well-executed procurement process, could be an appropriate countermeasure. But the more likely outcome is transfer of waste-filled government processes to private enterprises that operate their own waste-filled processes, in part because few leaders – whether in the private sector or municipal, state, and federal government – know much, if anything, about Lean management.

So where would the lower costs from privatization of government services come from? They'd come from the two usual sources:

- Reductions in wages and benefits for the private enterprise workers who deliver the services, and also likely from outsourcing certain tasks to subcontractors in low wage countries.

- Measuring unit cost savings – not total cost savings – a defective metric that is easily gamed and thus yields a misleading representation of the savings actually achieved (i.e. one that is far too optimistic) [2].

So what would we, as individuals and as a society, really gain? In most cases, it will turn out to be lower unit cost services that do not meet needs, resulting in higher total costs, as well as a lot of frustration among customers.

If I knew nothing about waste, as Taiichi Ohno defined it [3], then privatization of government services would seem like a great idea to me too. After all, isn't it an accepted fact that private enterprises can do anything a government can do, better, and at lower cost? Lean people, of course, like to question conventional wisdom. They would scrutinize the actual data and witness first-hand – "go see" – both government and private enterprise service processes before committing to such a comprehensive view.

Let's take a practical, real-world example: the post office. Government-run postal services in developed countries such as the United Kingdom, Germany, Japan, Canada and the United States face similar problems in recent years:

- Reduced volumes of first-class mail (the cash flow generator) due to the Internet

- Low shop floor and office worker productivity

- High costs (personnel, computer systems and automated machinery, fuel, retail outlets, etc.)

- Financial losses

- Greater customer expectations (less waiting in line for retail customer and lower costs for magazine publishers and other bulk mailing organizations)

How are postal services responding to these challenges? Since 1996, Canada Post has pursued the application of Lean principles and practices and has achieved remarkable results [4,5]. Japan Post will become privatized starting in October 2007, and has for the last few years been focused on process improvement led by consultants from Toyota Motor Corporation [6].

What about the U.S. Postal Service? They are taking a different approach to improve operational performance, one that is much more conventional and thus likely to yield conventional (i.e. mediocre) results. Their strategic plan is focused on responding to cost pressures, principally through standardization and innovation. They will invest in new equipment and technology, rationalize facilities, seek higher mail volumes from key customers, improve logistics, and outsource non-core competencies [7]. The plan also highlights the need for employee involvement and to improve the work environment.

Page 27 of the U.S. Postal Service's 96-page strategic plan says: "Quality control methods such as Six Sigma and Lean Management will be used to reduce variation and improve critical processes." This is the only place in the strategic plan that mentions Lean and Six Sigma. Further, the authors of the document – and likely most of postal service management – understand Lean management and Six Sigma narrowly, as quality improvement programs. This illustrates a depth of misunderstanding that will cause these important efforts to become another "flavor of the month."

If I knew nothing about kaizen, I'd think an organization's strategies, reports, and presentations would be an effective way to recognize problems, understand the true nature of problems, and identify effective solutions. But unfortunately, I do happen to know about kaizen and the power of genchi genbutsu – "go to the source to find the facts to make correct decisions" [8]. It seems that U.S. Postal Service executives need to improve their understanding of Lean management [9] – what "Continuous Improvement" and "Respect for People" really mean – and participate in kaizen [10]. Last time I checked,

U.S. Postal Service managers had not talked to Canada Post managers about their approach to operational improvement.

It is worth noting that some progress is being made at applying Lean principles and practices within some state and municipal government departments, including Connecticut's Department of Labor [11], Iowa's Department of Economic Development [12], and the City of Milwaukee's fleet services department [13].

What might be some other benefits of Lean principles and practices correctly applied to municipal, state, and federal government services? It could create a shared sense of purpose that all political parties and government departments can rally around; clearer and more consistent direction (both short- and long-term); improved information flows; better decision-making; fewer mistakes and re-work; reduce barriers for interacting with other people; better workplaces; provide better focus on the taxpaying customers' wants and needs; and help reduce costs.

Lean management could actually help give people what they want such as: right-sized government, lower taxes, effective security and strong defense, appropriate levels of funding for needed domestic and international activities, no-hassle services, better education for our children, and no spin.

Finally, it could deflate the unhealthy rhetoric that has plagued both the left and the right in recent decades, and bring weary citizens back into processes that identify and elect leaders, prioritize activities, and establish policy and laws. It could make politics more pleasant to participate in or follow, as the wasteful behaviors that add cost, but do not add value, dissipate. Does this sound like a crazy dream?

There would, of course, be many challenges to confront, including:

- Educating elected officials, appointed officials, and career government workers in Lean principles and practices, and ensuring they understand that Lean is not a program or initiative, or a means to lay people off.

- Turnover of elected and appointed officials every 2-4 years, and thus the need to train new leaders often [14].

- Making sure Lean efforts do not become ruined through politicization, labeling, misunderstanding, or misuse [15].

- Avoiding common Lean implementation errors [16].

These challenges suggest that Lean principles and practices should be taught much earlier than when most people become exposed to it – which is later in life, as adults in the workplace. We'd likely need to begin teaching Lean fundamentals as early as elementary school, and reinforcing those fundamentals through subsequent years of schooling.

An obvious question needs to be asked: "Why would any politician, appointed official, or career government worker risk doing something so different, so unfamiliar as Lean?" The answer is, to better serve their constituents – their tax-paying customers. But it's not likely much will happen until there is pull for Lean government from U.S. taxpayers, and until that pull is recognized and acted upon by government officials. Maybe someday it will happen, because it could become an absolute necessity.

Notes

[1] U.S. Department of Labor, Bureau of Labor Statistics, "BLS 2002-12 Labor Projections," http://stats.bls.gov/news.release/ecopro.t01.htm.

[2] M.L. Emiliani, D.J. Stec and L.P. Grasso, "Unintended Responses to a Traditional Purchasing Performance Metric," *Supply Chain Management: An International Journal*, Vol. 10, No. 3, 2005, pp. 150-156.

[3] T. Ohno, *Toyota Production System*, Productivity Press, Portland, OR, 1988.

[4] Steve Withers, "Process Excellence at Canada Post Corporation," presentation at the Lean Enterprise Institute Lean Service Summit, 23-24 June 2004, Amsterdam, The Netherlands.

[5] "Canada Post Puts Stamp on Lean Transformation," Lean Enterprise Institute, Brookline, MA, 2005, http://www.lean.org.

[6] *The Nikkei Weekly*, "POSTAL REFORM: Pursuit of Efficiency Thwarted by Failure of Privatization Bills," 18 August 2005.

[7] U.S. Postal Service, "Strategic Transformation Plan 2006-2010," http://www.usps.com/strategicplanning/2006-2010.htm.

[8] Toyota Motor Corporation, "The Toyota Way 2001," internal document, Toyota City, Japan, April 2001.

[9] B. Emiliani, with D. Stec, L. Grasso, and J. Stodder, *Better Thinking, Better Results: Case Study and Analysis of an Enterprise-Wide Lean Transformation, Second Edition*, The CLBM, LLC, Wethersfield, Conn., 2007.

[10] Always remember to apply the three principles of kaizen: process and results; system focus; non-blaming/non-judgmental. After M. Imai, "Kaizen Seminar", Hartford Graduate Center, Hartford, Conn., May 1988.

[11] T. Hutton, M. Stankiewicz, M., and J. Hasenjager, "Connecticut Department of Labor's Lean to Last Initiative," presentation given at the U.S. Department of Labor *Network '04 Conference*, South Portland, Maine, 3-5 November, 2004, http://www.doleta.gov/regions/reg01bos/trainingresources/2004/network04/learn2last.pdf.

[12] S. Baltes, "IDED Gets a Taste of Lean Enterprise," *Des Moines Business Record*, 20 February 2005, http://www.businessrecord.com/Main.asp?SectionID=8&SubSectionID=9&ArticleID=1688.

[13] V. Gupta, "Why Every Government Agency Should Embrace the Lean Process," *American Public Works Association Reporter*, April, 2004, http://www.apwa.net/

[14] Frequent turnover among middle managers and executives undermines Lean implementation efforts.

[15] Don't be surprised if some politicians try to use Lean as a Trojan horse to advance wasteful political rhetoric, agendas, or programs.

[16] M.L. Emiliani and D.J. Stec, "Leaders Lost in Transformation," *Leadership and Organizational Development Journal*, Vol. 26, No. 5, pp. 370-387, 2005

15 Lean Management for Non-Profits

Non-profit organizations can benefit tremendously by applying Lean principles and practices. And it could also have an enormous positive impact on fundraising activities.

It has taken nearly 15 years for Lean management to find its way into non-profit organizations - 501(c)(x) entities. Among the first to accept Lean have been healthcare organizations such as Virginia Mason Medical Center in Seattle and the University of Pittsburgh Medical Center.

Under immense scrutiny – regulatory, cost, safety, and quality of patient care – the leaders of some healthcare organizations have realized they must fundamentally re-think how they process information, interact with various stakeholders, and how they deliver services.

What about other non-profit organizations such as higher education, community development, human services, arts, or philanthropic organizations? Where are they when it comes to understanding and applying Lean principles and practices? Unfortunately, most are not even aware of it. There are many reasons for this, but three stand out:

- Leaders are anchored in the view that Lean is a "manufacturing thing," and therefore it does not apply to them.

- Most seem to associate Lean with negative outcomes such as layoffs or going out of business.

- They don't want to apply management techniques that could disrupt their business and negatively impact the services they provide.

The leaders of non-profit organizations are not the only people who have these negative perceptions of Lean management. However, it is important to understand negative perceptions are largely due to the actions of managers in for-profit business who have misunderstood and misapplied Lean principles and practices.

So why should the leaders and workers in non-profit organizations consider Lean management? Why should they invest any time or effort to reverse these deeply embedded negative perceptions? The reason is because there is something good in it for them and the people they serve, including:

- Better utilization of resources: time, money, labor, facilities, equipment, etc.
- Faster response to customers and other stakeholders
- Fewer errors and re-work
- Less stressful and more enjoyable workplace
- Better relationship with funding sources
- Less reporting and auditing headache

Lean management, done correctly, enables non-profits to fulfill their mission more effectively and better serve their customers. Applying Lean principles and practices will help uncover new resources from within existing means and enable non-profits to provide more of the current service or deliver new services.

The challenge for the leaders of non-profits is, of course, to understand and apply Lean correctly. While the two principles – "Continuous Improvement" and "Respect for People" – may appear to be simple, there is actually much to understand about each of them. But this should not be a deterrent. Rather, it should be seen as an attractive challenge that will lead to improved business processes and better outcomes for people.

16 How Lean Activities are Sabotaged

*Managers often try to limit or stop Lean efforts
championed by enthusiastic workers who occupy
lower-level positions. Exposing the specific
methods these managers use will enable
countermeasures to be devised.*

Managers who view Lean as a threat will usually try to shut
down Lean activities, particularly those initiated by people who
occupy lower levels in an organization. Their fears are driven
by mistakes in reasoning and illogical thinking [1]. These often
go unchallenged [2], which virtually guarantees such managers
will be successful in their efforts to derail Lean.

So the question is: How can resistance to Lean among mid-
and senior-level managers be overcome? One way is to
expose the specific methods employed by managers who
oppose the introduction of Lean management. This knowledge can then be used by Lean advocates to develop appropriate strategies and tactics for overcoming these methods.
The principal methods managers use to shut down Lean activities are:

Method 1:
Hide Behind Bureaucracy.

Examples of what managers say or do:
- "You'll need to meet with people in each of the depart-
  ments to get their buy-in."
- "There are Union issues that you'll need to address."

- "You need to determine how this could affect our certifications."
- "We need to form a committee to look at this."
- "This is not our current agenda."
- "Our metrics show there is no need for Lean."

Method 2:
Make False Claims, Mischaracterize, or Pigeonhole.

Examples of what managers say or do:
- Quietly tell influential people Lean won't work.
- "We're already doing that" or "We did that."
- Anchor potential participants with negative, incomplete, or inaccurate information about Lean management.
- "This will take a long time."
- "It's a program or initiative, same as Total Quality Management."
- "Lean is a manufacturing thing, and we're not a manufacturer."

Method 3:
Exercise Power via Bargaining, Indifference, or Inaction.

Examples of what managers say or do:
- Decision avoidance or string you along.
- "I'm the boss, and I say no."
- "There are other ways to achieve the same thing."
- Agree to do only one small pilot project.
- Threaten by signaling dire personal consequences if it does not work out.
- Boss is neither for it nor against it.
- Boss not available to meet to discuss Lean.

Method 4:
Initiate Long Cycle-Time Work or Re-Work Loops.

Examples of what managers say or do:
- Tell people they need to get more information or create a detailed plan.
- Ask people to prepare presentations, with detailed business case.
- "Show me who has done this in our industry."

Method 5:
Ask Questions That Emphasize Minutiae or Seek Highly Specific Answers; Ask Questions that are Ambiguous or Obfuscate.

Examples of what managers say or do:
- "Will this be effective? How will we know?"
- "Where's the proof that Lean works?"
- "What are the benefits?"
- "What are the measurable outcomes?"
- "What is the return on investment?"
- "How is this different from what we've been doing?"

Method 6:
Speculate Occurrence of Bad Outcomes.

Examples of what managers say or do:
- "This will hurt customer service."
- "This will be too disruptive."
- "The boss will never go for it."

Method 7:
Set People Up to Fail.

Examples of what managers say or do:
- Micro-manage activities.
- Not honoring commitments.
- Publicly proclaiming Lean is easy to do.
- Identifying a person to blame (i.e. "hold accountable") ahead of time.

Method 8:
Pressure a Specific Individual to Conform to the Current State.

Examples of what managers say or do:
- Make you feel like a bad person, or as if you have done something wrong.
- Make you feel that you are wrong, that you don't see things correctly, or are being subversive or insubordinate.
- Labeling person as difficult, not a team player, or disloyal.

Method 9:
Claim Resource Constraints.

Examples of what managers say or do:
- "We don't have budget for this."
- "We don't have time for this."
- "We don't have the people to do this."
- "We don't have the expertise."

Needless to say, it is not the role of management to shut down improvement efforts, and it is certainly not demonstrative of good leadership. Unfortunately, the threat these types of managers should be worried most about is themselves, not Lean. Time and energy are obviously better spent creating an improved future state than defending an inferior current state.

Can you think of two or three countermeasures for each of the nine methods?

Notes

[1] D. McInerny, *Being Logical: A Guide to Good Thinking*, Random House, New York, NY, 2005

[2] In some cases, the use of these nine methods is accompanied by bullying behaviors. This adds another challenging feature to the task of finding effective countermeasures. The general tactic for mitigating psychopathic behavior among managers is to recognize specific weaknesses and present a combination of ideas, information, evidence, etc., that play favorably to those weaknesses, thereby gaining acceptance. Alternatively, just ignore obstructionist managers and quietly carry out your Lean activities.

Afterword

I hope you have found these essays to be informative and brimming with practical information that you can immediately apply at work, particularly with regards to the "Respect for People" principle. While there is always much more to talk about, I'd like to briefly focus on three essays that I want you to remember because they are very important with regards to understanding and achieving REAL LEAN.

"Lean is Music to My Ears" captures a major challenge for senior managers which most do not address. Too many managers think they can simply bolt on Lean concepts learned at a one-day seminar to their existing knowledge base and succeed. That never works. Instead, managers, from CEO to supervisor have to practice Lean every day, just as professional musicians must practice playing music every day. The nature and scope of Lean practice will vary, from 5-day kaizens, to half-day kaizens, to small improvements in one's own work activities, to ensuring conversations with managers and associates always incorporate Lean principles and practices. This must happen every day, without exception.

"The Tragedy of Waste" helps us understand that business people long before our time had a pretty good understanding of waste and how to eliminate it. They also understood its unfavorable impact in the workplace and on the economic condition of company and country. This essay also helps us understand that, for about 100 years, it has been very difficult to get senior managers to pay attention to the waste and to directly participate in eliminating it. If you can get them interested, they will usually take shortcuts and adopt derivative forms of Lean that better fit their own needs and ideas. Unfortunately, this leaves in place, undisturbed, mountains of waste, unevenness, and unreasonableness. So please make a personal commitment to learn more and educate others about REAL LEAN, and avoid perpetuating the derivative forms of Lean that are inconsistent with the true practice and intent of Lean management.

This essay breaks new ground by asking that we consider if the adoption of Lean management is slowed by remnants of a negative left-leaning political characterization. Further, it is possible that many business leaders view Lean management as misaligned with the standard economic model that humans are rational self-interested maximizers. These two factors could help explain why most top managers adopt or create narrow derivative forms of Lean management that result in Fake Lean. Importantly, it is not difficult to identify elements of corporate, economic, or political theories that are inconsistent, in small or large ways, with the Lean management principles "Continuous Improvement" and "Respect for People."

"Too Much Selfish Thinking" takes us in a fresh new direction for understanding why so many derivative forms of Lean have appeared, and why, for many top leaders, REAL LEAN may not be appealing to them. Lean management is shown to be fundamentally rooted in the practical view that thoughtful sharing leads to greater prosperity and better outcomes. Promoting the desired reciprocal behaviors within the network of stakeholders starts by putting the "Respect for People" principle into daily practice. Doing so is an unselfish act that makes the other principle, "Continuous

Improvement," possible. To do this, we must accept that Lean is both learning and practice intensive.

The key challenge that emerges from this essay is to break free of the zero-sum thinking that underpins conventional management practice, and instead understand and pursue non-zero sum management practices. A related challenge is to understand utter practicality of non-zero sum management practices, as exemplified by Lean management, comprehend what it takes in terms of leadership beliefs and behaviors to access it, and then demonstrate the beliefs and behaviors at work every day. Once again, kaizen is the major pathway that leads to this awakening.

Finally, I return to the two Lean principles, "Continuous Improvement" and "Respect for People." The former is easy, while the latter takes years grasp. Just because it takes a long time to fully understand doesn't mean you shouldn't do it. You have the time and you have the intelligence. But do you have the motivation and the humility? And are you willing to challenge your assumptions and beliefs?

About the Author

 M.L. "Bob" Emiliani is a professor at Connecticut State University in New Britain, Conn., where he teaches various courses on Lean management.

He worked in the consumer products and aerospace industries for nearly two decades and held management positions in engineering, manufacturing, and sup-ply chain management, and had responsibility for implement-ing Lean in manufacturing operations and supply chains.

Emiliani has authored or co-authored a dozen papers related to Lean leadership including: "Lean Behaviors" (1998), "Linking Leaders' Beliefs to their Behaviors and Competencies" (2003), "Using Value Stream Maps to Improve Leadership" (2004), "Origins of Lean Management in America: The Role of Connecticut Businesses" (2006), and "Standardized Work for Executive Leadership (2008). Five of his papers have won awards for excellence.

He is the principal author of the book *Better Thinking, Better Results: Case Study and Analysis of an Enterprise-Wide Lean Transformation*, (second edition, 2007), a detailed case study and analysis of The Wiremold Company's Lean transforma-tion from 1991 to 2001. It won a Shingo Research Prize in 2003 as the first book to describe an enterprise-wide Lean transformation in a real company where both principles of Lean management – "Continuous Improvement" and "Respect for People" – were applied.

He is also the author of *REAL LEAN: Critical Issues and Opportunities in Lean Management* (Volume Two), published in 2007, *REAL LEAN: The Keys to Sustaining Lean Management* (Volume Three), published in 2008, and *Practical Lean Leadership: A Strategic Leadership Guide For Executives*, published in 2008.

Emiliani holds engineering degrees from the University of Miami, the University of Rhode Island, and Brown University.

He is the owner of The Center for Lean Business Management, LLC. (www.theclbm.com).

Made in the USA
San Bernardino, CA
17 March 2013